The Inside Scoop

TWO AGENTS DISH ON GETTING PUBLISHED

Janet Kobobel Grant and Wendy Lawton

Compiled by Olivia Butze

STORYARCHITECT
YOUR STORY | TOLD WELL

Published by Story Architect, 52 Mission Circle, Suite 122, PMB 170, Santa Rosa, CA 95409-5370

ISBN 978-0692834381

Cover Design by FaceOut Studio
Interior design and typeset by Katherine Lloyd, the DESK

To Mr. B
with deepest thanks

Contents

PART THREE
THE INSIDE SCOOP ON PRESENTING YOUR IDEA TO AN AGENT

PART FOUR
THE INSIDE SCOOP ON YOUR PROPOSAL AND QUERY

PART FIVE
THE INSIDE SCOOP ON HOW THE AUTHOR AND THE AGENT WORK TOGETHER

PART SIX
THE INSIDE SCOOP ON CONTRACTS AND BEING PAID FOR YOUR WORK

PART SEVEN
THE INSIDE SCOOP ON WHAT HAPPENS AFTER YOUR BOOK IS CONTRACTED

PART EIGHT
THE INSIDE SCOOP ON MARKETING STRATEGIES THAT WILL SELL COPIES OF YOUR BOOK

PART NINE
AT LONG LAST! THE INSIDE SCOOP ON YOUR BOOK LAUNCH

PROLOGUE

The Scoop

Here's the scoop: Undertaking to write a book is no small task, and seeing that book through the publishing process isn't for the faint of heart either.

Fortunately, guides are available for the adventure. The two of us, seasoned veterans of the publishing industry, will walk with you through the steps from the germination of a book idea to the day you host your first publicity event with your finished book in hand—and the highlights in between.

Some of the questions we'll answer are:

- What makes an idea publishable?
- How do you decide between independent and traditional publishing?
- How do you present your idea to an agent or publisher?
- What elements are in a proposal?
- What makes a literary agent say yes to representing you?
- What do you need to know about contracts and being paid for your work?
- What happens after your book is contracted?
- What marketing strategies work to sell copies of your book?

Hang onto your hat! This isn't a leisurely cruise but a ride down the white water rapids of the publishing world.

The Inside Scoop on What Makes a Book Publishable

CHAPTER 1

Let's Talk Basics

By Janet Kobobel Grant

The most fundamental aspect of publishing your book is whether you have an idea that genuinely would interest others. Without that core, solid idea, you're not ready to publish, either as an independent or with a traditional publisher.

To determine if your idea is book worthy, test it by asking these questions:

- *Is it a book or an article?* Often, when a writer has an idea, the first thought that springs to mind is to write a book. But sometimes the notion isn't weighty enough to be a book. It might be more suited to an article or a series of blogs, or if it's fiction, to a short story.
- *Is the idea multi-layered enough to warrant a book?* Play with the concept for a while and run through your head (or on paper) just how much material you have.
- *Would a reader want to buy a book on your idea?* Several years ago, if a parent discovered her child had diabetes, she would head to the bookstore to buy a cookbook for diabetics, a book to understand diabetes better, a book on parenting a diabetic child, and a children's book to help her offspring understand diabetes. Today, a parent goes online to find all those materials, including help on how to talk to her child about the disease.

The writer should then ask these questions: *Where else might a potential reader find this same material? What would cause a reader to buy a book with my material?*

- *What's the competition?* When a brilliant idea lights up in your brain, before you get too carried away, realize you're unlikely to be the first person to have come up with it. Check around online to see what other books already exist that would be competition for your idea.

  If you see that Bill Bryson wrote something similar two years ago, you should either explore your idea on your blog or quietly set it aside, knowing you can't compete with a top-selling, well-established author's book. While that might seem like a straightforward decision to make, I've observed it's very hard for writers to be realistic about the competition. I guess we all want to see our idea as unique. When I ask an author I represent if he has checked out the competition, it's not unusual for me to hear this response, "Yeah, Bryson wrote about the same topic, but I'm focusing my book differently." Potential book buyers don't take a close enough look at both books to discern the subtly differentiated focus. They see Bill Bryson wrote about topic A. Now you've written about topic A. Book-buying decision made.

In addition to asking yourself the above questions, you have to keep your idea *fresh*, which Wendy will explore in Chapter 2.

CHAPTER 2

Is Your Idea Fresh?

By Wendy Lawton

You've heard it over and over. Agents and publishers receive a staggering number of manuscripts. If I were a writer trying to catch a break, this information might be enough to stop me in my tracks. The odds are overwhelmingly against the writer. But that fact by itself is not enough information.

The truth is that much of what we in the publishing industry see is the same old, same old. Something fresh, however, stands out.

So what do I mean by fresh? Let me try to explain.

Fiction: Fresh Idea

If you could see the material writers send us agents, you would realize that we get the same concepts over and over. Yes, there is a limited number of plots told in different ways–someone posited that there are only seven basic plots: man vs. nature, man vs. man, man vs. the environment, man vs. machines/technology, man vs. the supernatural, man vs. self, and man vs. God/religion. But when you add the creativity of the writer to a basic plot, the possibilities are endless. Come up with something new, something we would love to read, and you will be in a small minority. Sometimes when you blend two genres, you come up with something fresh.

Take the British television drama *Endeavor*. Yes, it's ostensibly another cop show, but it's a standout because the creators actually took a beloved character, Inspector Morse, and gave us a prequel. *Endeavor* is the previously unknown first name of Morse. We get to see the backstory, which is at least as interesting as the original drama. They've combined the city of Oxford with its varied academic settings and Morse's unusual path to police work with complicated, fascinating characters and non-cliché murder scenarios. Fresh. No wonder it's gained such a large, loyal following.

Fiction: Fresh Writing

If you've read the best-seller *The Help*, you'll understand why it stood out from the rest. The author's voice, combined with a compelling story and unforgettable characters, made this book exceptional.

It's impossible to give instructions for writing in a fresh manner, but we sure recognize fresh writing when we see it. The more you read, the more you will recognize it as well. And reading good books, fresh books, starts to infiltrate your own writing. You develop your voice by osmosis, not by technique.

Fiction: Fresh Characters

This is key to writing standout fiction. We tend to first gravitate toward creating stereotypes. As one editor told me, "The wise older slave woman in Southern historical fiction has become a stereotype."

The writer who wants to create fresh characters has to walk a fine line–give us someone new but don't give us someone we can't identify with. I see a lot of women's fiction writers who decide to have a male main character–it's different, after all. Different, but not good. If you write women's fiction, the protagonist almost always should be a woman (or alternating points of view between the hero and heroine).

Nonfiction: Untapped Need

If you can marry your own expertise with an untapped need or a fascinating subject, you will have a winner on your hands. Think of Malcolm Gladwell's books. He answers the questions we all think about: What makes something become an overnight success? (*The Tipping Point.*) Why do some people exceed all expectations? (*Outliers.*)

Or look at Brennan Manning's *Ragamuffin Gospel*, written "for the bedraggled, beat-up, and burnt-out." In his review of the book, author Max Lucado said, "Brennan Manning does a masterful job of blowing the dust off of shop-worn theology." That's fresh.

Nonfiction: Fresh Format

Sometimes the thing that makes a book fresh is when the author comes up with a new way to present the information. I've been fascinated by the wildly popular use of adult coloring books to present nonfiction subjects in an interactive way. This trend peaked in 2015–2016 and showcased publishers realizing just how many people learn from a tactile modality. Put a colored pencil in their hands, and they interact with the information in a whole new way. This is also the reason you'll see many books with sidebars, pull-quotes and more complicated interior design. Those capture the visual learners.

Nonfiction: Fresh Voice

When we agents come across a fresh voice in nonfiction, it immediately catches our attention. Can you imagine a fresh voice in a grammar manual? Neither could I until I read *Woe Is I* by Patricia T. O'Connor. I mean, she talks about the limitations of language like this: "If English weren't so stretchy and unpredictable, we wouldn't have Lewis Carroll, Dr. Seuss, or the Marx brothers. And just try telling a knock-knock joke in Latin!" You've got to love it.

Memoir is all about voice. Examples of fresh voices would be Jeannette Walls in *The Glass Castle* and Haven Kimmel's *A Girl Named Zippy*.

How do you know if it's fresh? Stalk bookstore shelves. Research on Amazon. Read publishers' websites. Ask a librarian. Read everything you can in your genre. Talk with other writers. Again, it takes research. An idea formulated in a vacuum may be a result of *zeitgeist*—just like a hundred other ideas, all hatched at the same time.

What are the dangers of trying to be fresh? This is where it takes real instinct. Trying to be different can lead to something odd, something quirky, something that doesn't work because it's too different.

I wish I could give you a concrete formula like 25 percent fresh, 75 percent comfortable. But of course that's impossible. It's up to you to try out an idea and let others chime in. Here's where the combination of your art and knowledge are put to the test, where the strength of your writing really lies.

And that leads us to think about the writing rules and when to follow them, when to break them.

CHAPTER 3

Strong Writing: Following the Rules

By Wendy Lawton

If you've been part of a writing group, whether online or in person, no doubt you've heard the bedrock rules for fiction.

Show, don't tell.

No backstory in the first umpteen pages.

No flashbacks in children's fiction.

Stay away from prologues.

As someone who reads an inordinate number of manuscripts each year, I can assure you that these rules are meant as guidelines only. When slavishly followed, they lead to all kinds of problems.

So what's a writer to do?

The answer is simple: Honor the story, but don't be a slave to rules. Each one of those rules is meant to help you write a better story, but goose-stepping to a set of rules can suck the very life out of your writing. Let me take just one oft-repeated rule and examine it.

Show, don't tell. You've heard this hundreds of times. It's repeated so often because it's good advice but only up to a point. What it means is that instead of telling us the story, the good writer will show it—letting it unfold before our eyes. It's so much more immediate.

Unfortunately, I see too many manuscripts where the adage is taken to the limit. Every minute detail is shown. Every emotion is carefully etched on every character's face—in the droop of his shoulders, the shuffle of his feet. Even walk-on characters are named and shown in excruciating detail. There is precious little narrative, just scene after scene.

By the third page, the reader is worn out. The story is overwritten, overwrought. I tend to put this kind of manuscript down by the end of the first page.

A skillful writer knows that you *tell* the parts you want to speed up. You *show* the significant parts. The careful balance of the two will move the story along. Showing is the way you focus the reader's attention. It's like taking the reader's face in your hands and aiming it toward the important elements of the story. If you take that face and aim it all over the place, your reader will end up with literary whiplash. The art comes in the perceptive use of both showing and telling. It's all about pacing and highlighting.

When are other times you would want to tell? If you want to artistically handle violent scenes, use a judicious telling instead of showing. Your gentle reader will bless you. The same is true for overtly sexual scenes. If your genre does not call for sexuality, those scenes can be told with taste and artful omission. The next time you're critiqued by a neophyte rule-follower who smugly points out every instance of telling in your manuscript, I want you to be able to explain why you used telling in some places and showing in others.

That's just one fiction rule we've debunked. The more you read fine fiction, the more you will see that every rule can be broken with impunity in the hands of a *skillful novelist.* Just don't assume that mantle before you're ready to wear it well.

CHAPTER 4

Strong Writing: Where to Begin Your Book

By Janet Kobobel Grant

Obviously we need to begin our creative piece in a way that's suited to its category. But sometimes we aren't as intentional in constructing that first sentence or first paragraph as we should be. Let's explore where to begin various types of writing.

A Novel

In fiction, the very best books nab us by the collar and whip us into the story in the first sentence. *Gone Girl* is superbly written even though it's a disturbing storyline.

Here's the opener: "When I think of my wife, I always think of her head." That's kind of odd, right? Not many men would say that. I'm nabbed.

The opening to Laura Frantz's historical novel *Love's Reckoning*: "'Twas time for his daughters to wed, Papa said. But he had a curious way of bringing wedded bliss about, sending all the way to Philadelphia for a suitor." I want to know more!

A Nonfiction Book

I checked out some of the nonfiction books I've enjoyed and found that most of them, regardless of category, start with a story. It takes a while for the book's purpose to unfold. Unlike fiction, we are drawn in more slowly to the book.

Here's the start to *The End of Money: Counterfeiters, Preachers, Techies, Dreamers—and the Coming Cashless Society* by David Wolman: "On Christmas Eve 2009, Umar Farouk Abdulmatallab began the journey he thought would take him from this world into the next, and into the awaiting embrace of six dozen virgins." That's a startling opening sentence! The author goes on to tell us about the underwear bomber who fumbled his chance at infamy and those virgins. What's that have to do with the end of money? Turns out the terrorist bought his ticket for that ride to heaven using cash. Yup, he bought a one-way ticket from Lagos, Nigeria, to Detroit, using $2,381.

The book's thesis is established through story and then stated directly on page 2: "Money is no object. [Referring to the bomber.] Maybe so for a lucky few. Except, of course, money is an object—tearable, flammable, even wearable." Wolman thus begins his exploration of what money is, why we use it, and what would it mean to end using it.

Now, take a look at the beginning to *The Immortal Life of Henrietta Lacks*: "There's a photo on my wall of a woman I've never met, its left corner torn and patched together with tape. She looks straight into the camera and smiles, hands on hips, dress suit neatly pressed, lips painted deep red. It's the late 1940s, and she hasn't yet reached the age of thirty. Her light brown skin is smooth, her eyes still young and playful, oblivious to the tumor growing inside her—a tumor that would leave her five children motherless and change the future of medicine."

That opening sets up a fascinating read as the author braids the woman's life story around the effect that tumor has had on medicine and each of our lives. That complex interplay between the personal and the scientific continues throughout the book. The author has established how she will approach the book and the book's purpose with clear intent at the outset.

So where should you begin your book? Generally a novel starts with a point of contention or curiosity, and a nonfiction piece begins with a story (or a quote or statistic) that establishes the theme and the tone of the book.

After that, as I explain in the next chapter, structure is a key way to keep your audience hooked.

CHAPTER 5

Strong Writing: Beyond the First Page

By Janet Kobobel Grant

Once a reader makes it beyond the first page, strong structure sustains his or her interest. Recently I was looking over the table of contents for a project one of my clients was creating. It seemed really complex, and I was struggling to see why the ideas were strung together as they were.

Then, in the middle of the manuscript, I saw a chapter in which the author shows that the problem being examined has roots in childhood. Ah-ha! That's where the book needs to begin, with the root of the problem.

Often the best structure, especially for a nonfiction book, is linear—start at the beginning. If you're writing a personal story about a life-changing event, usually the best way to tell the narrative is from start to finish.

Sometimes writers become caught up in wanting to structure their books with bells and whistles and special flourishes. But that can lead to gilding the lily. Let the lily of your manuscript remain unadorned by doodads that just make it look fussy rather than beautiful. For example, I had a client who decided to frame her nonfiction self-help book around the life cycle of a frog. Don't ask me why. It *might* have worked, but she used so many references to said frog that the analogy grew tiresome. Enough already about the frog! Just give us a simple structure that has clean lines.

Fiction, too, can be fraught with peril in where to begin. **One of the most common problems with a novel is that it starts in the wrong place—oftentimes in backstory.** As I've pondered why writers make this mistake regularly, I've concluded that the author is so caught up in what makes the character respond to the story's major conflict that the writer thinks the reader will want to know that info right up front to make the protagonist sympathetic. But motivations should be woven in bit-by-bit, not handed to the reader by fistfuls at the outset.

Draw us in through the conflict, not through motivations. And if your novel isn't coming together as well as you had hoped, drop the first two chapters. Or even start in the middle of the novel rather than where you began it initially. Chances are, the middle is the perfect place to begin.

And speaking of middles…

CHAPTER 6

Strong Writing: Sagging Middles

By Janet Kobobel Grant

Shakespeare noted, "There's many a slip twixt the cup and the lip." How true when it comes to writing. You might start off your manuscript with a bang and know that the conclusion is solid. But many a book has been undone by its sagging middle.

Have you created a book that holds the reader on tenterhooks throughout? The middle of the book is treacherous territory because you have to create enough tension and interest to keep the reader engaged until the end.

The most obvious mistake in a novel that leads to a hammock-like middle is lackluster plotting. If your characters are just going through the paces of what was established at the beginning of the book, the middle droops. If the writer isn't sure how to quicken the pace but is simply marking time (and word count) until the dramatic conclusion, the middle won't be interesting.

But other, subtler problems can cause the reader to wonder why he or she should keep reading.

Avoid Changing the POV

An example of a novel that failed to keep good pacing, in my opinion, is Kathryn Stockett's *The Help*. In the middle of the book, the author made a move that stopped the novel's pacing dead in its tracks. The scene is a gala event that all of the novel's main characters will attend. The tension is running high at this point, and the reader realizes that the characters' actions have brought them to a pivotal point of major conflict. So I entered the middle of the novel with anticipation.

But the author chose—for this one scene in the book—to move into the omniscient point of view. As a reader, that effectively disengaged me from everything that happened in the scene. Suddenly I've been transported from seeing events from either the point of view of the black hired help or from the point of view of one white woman to, in effect, being plopped up on a balcony overlooking the room and watching each character fall apart in her own way. But I didn't care! All the energy was drained from the scene by removing me from the interiors of the characters.

Avoid Using a New Writing Device

Another novel that has, in my opinion, a flaw in the middle is *The Madonnas of Leningrad*. This story takes place in the Hermitage during the siege of Leningrad during World War II. The museum is being guarded by those who worked at the Hermitage to save it from destruction. The workers are starving to death, as is everyone in the city.

The protagonist is on the roof of the museum, reporting any fires started from German bombs. Suddenly the novel moves into magical realism, which we haven't seen in the first portion of the book, nor will we see anywhere else, and a statue of a Greek god comes to life, rapes the protagonist and leaves her pregnant—a virtual madonna of Leningrad.

As a reader I was unprepared for this pivotal scene because it seemed to have been dropped into the midst of the book as if from some other novel. Now, if the author had used magical realism earlier, this scene would have made sense. But standing apart from the rest of the novel while certainly shining a spotlight on this important scene, the chapter turned out to be disruptive to the book's flow. (I thought the book was masterful on so many levels that this misstep was especially disappointing.)

Why did these two authors, who wrote such strong books, make what

I consider mistakes? I think they were working too hard to make sure the middle of their novels didn't sag.

I've used fiction examples because it's more challenging to maintain reader interest in the middle of a novel than a nonfiction book. And, unless the category is narrative nonfiction or memoir, the nonfiction reader can skip hither and yon, skimming some parts or turning directly to the section that interests him or her. Still, lessons can be learned from these middles for both the novelist and the nonfiction writer.

- Realize that you make promises to the reader in the first part of your book about what to expect throughout. Keep your promises.
- If you plan a significant scene in the middle of your book (which is a good way to keep it from sagging), plant the seed for that scene rather than abruptly changing course.
- Keep in mind the importance of creating an arc in your book, even with nonfiction, so the reader has a sense of increasing conflict as the book unfolds.

However you decide to keep your book's momentum, make sure the approach is authentic. Unique ideas, such as planting an icon early on in the text to support a significant middle scene, can do wonders as well.

CHAPTER 7

Strong Writing: When a Book Ends Badly

By Janet Kobobel Grant

We can all recall the moment a film ended poorly, a TV show's closing didn't satisfy, or a book's conclusion just felt like a cheat.

One example of a book that had stepped lively and well until the end is Leif Enger's *Peace Like a River.* The end of the book *really* comes when the father dies. Written powerfully, this scene leaves the reader stunned by the rapturous conclusion of his life, as he's swept into a figuratively peaceful river. However, because the author has left many important story strings dangling, he must tie them up.

At this point, the novel drifts off rather than ending solidly. It's as if Enger realized: 1) his deadline was upon him, and he had better just rush through and tie up the loose ends; or 2) he already had exceeded his word count and needed to just end the thing; or 3) he was impatient for the creative process to be over so he ran pell-mell to the last sentence.

Why do I say the ending was unsatisfactory? Because it's a summary that goes on for pages and pages—a seeming eternity to me. We're told what happens rather than shown. It's almost a synopsis of the conclusion rather than the real deal.

The Help also has a rushed feel with its ending. Skeeter's mother miraculously recovers from her cancer so Skeeter can move to New York, and Celia Foote, a character the reader has come to care about, is dropped about three-fourths of the way through the novel with no resolution to her concerns. *Most* of the story's threads are sewn into the conclusion and lead to a satisfying ending. It was so close to perfection but didn't quite make the mark.

In nonfiction, leaving the reader with a sense of satisfaction is also important. Here's the conclusion to Jon Meacham's *American Lion: Andrew Jackson in the White House*: "The eyes of Jackson's statue look south, across the Potomac River and toward the pockets of rebellion he put down—keeping watch, never blinking, never tiring. 'He still lives in the bright pages of history,' Stephen Douglas said in dedicating the statute. *He still lives*—and we live in the country he made, children of a distant and commanding father, a father long dead yet ever with us." Sounds solid, doesn't it? Nicely wrapped up, bringing the book full circle and reminding the reader of Meacham's perspective on why Jackson was so important to our country.

What can we learn, as writers, from those endings that disappointed us?

- **Don't kill off a beloved character before his/her time.** I think an author can end a character's life if the reader has time to adjust to the inevitability of it. The point is to have an artistic purpose for doing so. Otherwise, death can feel like a cheat, an easy answer to a writing problem, as opposed to a natural outcome of where the storyline was going. When it comes to doing away with a major character, it seems almost a kindness to let him or her slip away while on the job, but not killed by a murderous rogue or a violent car accident right after a joyous moment (my thoughts are drifting to Matthew Crawley's death via car accident in the Downton Abbey TV series). "Let the reader down gently" might be the best advice. Unless, of course, you're writing a gritty story; then a violent ending suits the genre.

- **Leave readers with a sense of anticipation.** Let the reader imagine some hopeful future for your characters, that they've grown in a significant way, and even though the upcoming days will have their challenges, the characters are ready to face them.
- **Even if you're tired of your characters, never let the reader guess.**
- **Keep the plotline fresh.**
- **Avoid neat bows at the end.** If you write a series, enter into the plotting process for your last book realizing that tying bows on each plot point in the last chapter isn't satisfying or even all that interesting to the reader. Allow some characters to exit the stage before the very end. If you're writing a single title, you're unlikely to have as much to wrap up, but give us a sense that the story is starting to wind down before the last few pages.

CHAPTER 8

Salable Writing: Hot Buttons, Hot Books

By Janet Kobobel Grant

One aspect of a manuscript that makes it salable is hitting readers' hot buttons. If a book doesn't shout out to the potential reader, "You need me!" that reader is going to bypass the book and snatch up the one sitting on the proverbial shelf next to it.

What do I mean by hot buttons?

For fiction, a hot button usually is an idea that tickles the reader's fancy. Take, for example, my decision to read *Room by* Emma Donoghue. Why did I pick that novel out of the plethora available? I found out about the book while rummaging around on Amazon for a new book to read. Amazon recommended *Room* to me, so I checked out what the plot was about: A young woman is kidnapped and held against her will for years by a man who regularly rapes her. She has a baby boy as a result.

I felt ambivalent about the story. Would it be too dark? Would it be offensive? Would it be disturbing?

But I noted that the book had received significant reviews from others who tended to like books that I, too, enjoyed. So I started to lean toward giving it a try.

I also remembered a young woman in the Los Angeles area who had, in real life, experienced a similar kidnapping. I had been fascinated by the thought of what her life had been like for all those years of captivity and how her life would always be marked by that jolting disruption to normalcy. Maybe *Room* would explore some of the questions that I had about such an event.

What tipped the scale for me was the reader reviews on Amazon. Others had found the book not only satisfying but enriching and oddly life-affirming.

Coming back to that hot button idea: I might not have read the book if I hadn't connected it to an event I had followed in the news.

For nonfiction, hot buttons are more felt needs rather than intellectual curiosity. We want certain things in our lives—health, peace, money, more friends, less fat. We want to be smarter, fitter, "in the know." Whatever people *want* certainly fits into the hot button category, but hot buttons are more complex than that. I might want to read about race in America, but I also want a book that has a unique twist to a perennial topic. That's one of the reasons that, in the middle of discussions brought on by the Black Lives Matter movement, *Between the World and Me* by Ta-Nehisi Coates lured many a reader in.

Winner of the Pulitzer Prize and the National Book Award, named one of the 10 Best Books of the Year, it took a different sort of look at race. Here is how the publisher describes the book's approach: "What is it like to inhabit a black body and find a way to live within it? And how can we all honestly reckon with this fraught history and free ourselves from its burden?

"*Between the World and Me* is Ta-Nehisi Coates's attempt to answer these questions in a letter to his adolescent son. Coates shares with his son—and readers—the story of his awakening to the truth about his place in the world through a series of revelatory experiences, from Howard University to Civil War battlefields, from the South Side of Chicago to Paris, from his childhood home to the living rooms of mothers whose children's lives were taken as American plunder."

The result? A book that hit readers' hot button and became a hot book because it examined a complex issue with boldness, honesty, insight and tenderness toward the author's son—and thereby toward the reader.

A book that accomplishes that is like a writer snapping his fingers in front of an agent or an editor—you will get our attention.

But even more important than asking what is hot now is the question, "What will be hot two years from now?" If you contracted to write a book today, it would likely release in two years (one year to write the book and one year for the publisher to produce it, set up a marketing plan, and sell it into outlets). Unless, of course, you decide to self-publish, which is an option we'll explore in Part Two.

Meanwhile, let's look beyond hot buttons to the decisions you make about genre, title, how you want to be thought of as an author, and other issues that either make your manuscript attractive to a publisher (and readers) or not.

CHAPTER 9

Salable Writing: To Thy Own Book Be True

By Janet Kobobel Grant

I'm struck by how often writers don't know where their books would fit on a bookstore's shelves. Yeah, yeah, I know that we're pretty much talking virtual shelves. And that you don't care *which* shelf, just so it's on a shelf.

But it *does* matter where it would go. Thinking in terms of real shelves in a real bookstore helps us to realize that sometimes a writer creates a book that's neither beast nor fowl. It's not exactly a memoir that centers on grief yet it's not exactly a prescriptive book on grief. A manuscript needs to be true to its kind. It must be one thing or the other so the agent who reads it knows what it is; the editor who receives it from the agent knows what it is; the editor can explain what it is to marketing/sales/management; the marketing folks can explain in the catalog, back cover copy and press releases what it is; the sales staff can tell the bookstore buyer what it is…so it reaches the appropriate reader. If the cycle breaks down at the writer's stage, it's unlikely to make it to the end of cycle.

How do you know where your book would fit in a bookstore? Might I suggest you mosey down to your local bookstore? (Or make a major trek, if necessary, to find one.) Wander around, and look for books similar to yours. Where are they shelved? And take a peek at back covers. Publishers have standard categories that tell bookstores where to shelve the book. The answer to your question is printed on the backs of other books.

My point is simple but important: Choose a category and make sure your book stays true to the qualities necessary to neatly fit–smack dab in the center–of a category.

Another factor that makes your writing salable is your clear understanding of the market.

CHAPTER 10

Salable Writing: Know the Market Realities

By Wendy Lawton

When deciding what you'll write, the tack you'll take, and how long your book will be, think through the market realities. It will help you to avoid a lot of rejection from agents and editors.

For a boost in getting started, here are some writers' laments and agents' responses to those laments that offer insights.

Writers' Laments:

- **Lament One:** *I've written my first book. It's not only fresh and well-written, but I've experimented with technique and really pushed the envelope when it comes to content and format. My critique group calls it a work of literary genius. So why can't I get anyone interested in it?*
- **Lament Two:** *Every time the critique group gets together it has begun to feel like a lesson in futility. Another writer–an excellent writer–writes generational historical fiction. Her characters are well-drawn and her plots are multi-layered. These are big books, about 200,000 words each. Blood, sweat and tears have gone into*

each book, but do you think she's been able to sell a single title to a publisher?

- **Lament Three:** *A newer member writes children's books. Again, these are good–really good by any standard–based on her great-grandmother's life. These books read just like* Little House on the Prairie. *However, they are not selling.*
- **Lament Four:** *Even our nonfiction writers keep getting passed over. We have one pastor who packs out the church each Sunday with his sermons. He's compiled these into a book–kind of The Best of Pastor Miller. These are tried and tested messages. It sounds like a no-brainer for a publisher, right? Wrong. He can't get a bite despite having attended a writers conference.*

Agents' Responses:

- **Lament One:** I received this proposal and just sent out a rejection. There were indications the writer could write, and the plot was intriguing, but the technique was so showy the story took a back seat to the fancy footwork. Why do writers get so caught up in trying to write a book that will impress their creative writing professors? That's a mighty small audience. Besides, a new author needs to gain a readership and the trust of those readers before he or she ever attempts to push into uncharted waters. Why do so many new writers long to push the envelope? Why not just write a great, commercially-viable book? That's what I can sell to a publisher, and that's what publishers can sell to bookstores. That's the book readers want to buy. Such a shame.
- **Lament Two:** I love historical fiction but 200,000 words? It shows me this writer doesn't understand the market. Yes, Ken Follett might be able to get away with a book of this heft, but it would be the kiss of death for a debut author. Books are priced mainly based on what it costs to produce and print the book. Why would someone buy an unknown author's trade paper book for the same price they could get the newest Janet

Evanovich hardcover? Book length is a simple matter of economics. A new author shoots herself in the foot with a book that is twice as long as other books in the genre.

- **Lament Three:** *Little House on the Prairie* is a classic. It was written a long time ago, and though we still love to read the series, styles change even in children's books. An editor does not want to see a clone of an age-old classic; he or she wants to see a book written for a twenty-first century audience. Too often children's books are written for some idealized child reader, more like the children the author remembers from childhood. These sentimental books rarely find a home.
- **Lament Four:** Not another book of transcribed sermons or talks! The written word is far different from the spoken word. Creating a nonfiction book requires planning, a story arc, stories to illustrate the concepts, and features–not to mention a compelling idea that hasn't already been tackled.

While these agents' responses may worry you, keep in mind that they can be easily avoided if you take the time to do your homework. Know what's working in the marketplace in terms of word count, writing style and approach that suits today, not yesteryear.

CHAPTER 11

Salable Writing: Choosing Your Genre

By Janet Kobobel Grant

What makes a novelist pick a certain genre in which to write? What makes someone with a yen to write a nonfiction book pick a certain category? Here are a few reasons that occur to me:

- The writer likes to read a certain type of book. If you're hooked on romances, it makes sense you'd like to write one. If you are drawn to memoir, you can picture yourself writing your story that way.
- The genre is revered. Writing literary fiction or a work of social significance sounds erudite.
- The category is popular. Harry Potter books set off a whirlwind of imitators; *Heaven Is for Real* caused editors to seek out others who experienced heaven and returned to earth to tell us about it.
- The writer can't envision writing his or her book any other way. Sometimes a book idea arrives in a rush of creativity, neatly labeled in a certain category.

Why do genre and categories matter to publishers? Here are several reasons I have observed over the last few decades.

- Genres fall in and out of publishing favor. It hasn't been that long since publishers didn't want to touch a personal story unless the writer was a big name. Today, people with exquisite writing skills can recount a segment of their lives in a memoir and end up with numerous publishers vying to publish the book. Or another ordinary person can decide to take a year living unplugged and then write about it in the form of narrative nonfiction.
- Writers have a voice that works in one genre but not in another. If a novelist writes in short, terse sentences, suspense is probably a natural but romance probably is not.
- Category affects a book's structure and tone. If you want to write about the history of salt (which is a fascinating story, by the way), you could write with a scientific bent, which would be pretty technical, or you could follow the timeline of salt's influence on politics, or recount the story of salt's effect on societies, or you could even write about salt through an epic novel (just think what James Michener could have done with that idea!). Each approach brings with it a natural tone and a structure for the book that makes sense. And even though salt is the topic for all these approaches, each way of writing about it would put the book in a different category.
- Readers of your genre launch into your book with a sharply defined set of expectations. These readers might not even realize such is the case, but disappointment is bound to ensue should you not deliver. In these moments of mistaken identity, a rose by any other name does not smell as sweet.
- If you mislabel your submission, you're showing you most certainly can't meet the category requirements.
- Likewise, astute agents know the difference between one genre and another and might immediately eliminate your query if you show you don't know the distinction.

How do you decide?

- Know what categories exist in your chosen arena of fiction or nonfiction. If you don't know your options, you can hardly make an informed choice. If you don't know the difference between a mystery and a suspense (see the next chapter where I explain the difference) or between memoir and narrative nonfiction, how will you decide the best fit for your idea?

- Stay current with what's showing up in the market. If one book (or series) hits really big, it's unlikely publishers will buy manuscripts to compete with something that's selling well. For example, when *The Shack* blew past all other books on the fiction best-seller list, that wasn't a good time to write an allegory. Readers were unlikely to rush out to buy a ton of allegories; they wanted to hear more from *The Shack*'s author, William P. Young.
- Keep up with the best-seller lists that reflect your potential readers' interests so you can track longer-range trends. A lively market for a genre, as opposed to a single work, is an indication of an arena that might stay perky for a while. Historical romance was the hot ticket for several years, but the glut of novels in that genre shifted the focus to suspense. Next year the shift could be to a genre nobody foresaw as becoming popular. The trick, of course, is that shifts can occur suddenly. You can put your energies into writing a certain category, only to discover publishers have overbought in it just about the time you are ready to show off your work.
- To thy own self be true. The bottom line—always has been, always will be—is to listen to your instincts. If you're comfortable writing in a category, don't abandon it to follow the crowds. Writing a wonderful book occurs when you write with passion and compassion—for your characters and for your belief in your idea.

What happens if you choose the wrong genre for your writing? I think we can be pretty confident that the manuscript will never reach its potential if you make a genre misstep. A story that would have unfolded beautifully as a historical novel might fall flat as a contemporary. A nonfiction book that could have resonated with many as a memoir might never develop word-of-mouth enthusiasm as an investigative expose. So study up on the characteristics of the genre you want to write in, decide if it still seems like a good fit, and then write within the boundaries established for that genre. No fancy footwork or taking a divergent path.

CHAPTER 12

Salable Writing: Mystery vs. Suspense, How to Know the Difference

By Janet Kobobel Grant

Two of the most confused genres are mystery and suspense. So I've detailed what characteristics differ between the two. Hopefully these tips will help you when labeling your work—and figuring out how to write the story.

In suspense, the reader anxiously waits for something to happen: A bomb is set to go off, a bank robbery is about to occur, a deadly virus is about to be released. Generally, the protagonist is aware of the impending danger and attempts to divert it from happening. The outcome is *suspended* until the end of the book, as the protagonist rushes to subvert the tragedy.

In a mystery, the catastrophe has happened or occurs at the book's outset: The bomb has gone off, the bank has been robbed, the virus has been unleashed…or more commonly, someone has been murdered. The protagonist solves the puzzle of who did the deed by tracing through how the crime was carried out and eliminating suspects—sometimes while the perpetrator creates additional havoc.

In suspense, the action tends to be physical, and the reader knows who committed the crime—and often why.

In a mystery, the action tends to be mental as the protagonist (and the reader!) tries to solve the puzzle and figure out why the crime was committed. As in true crime, readers of mysteries want to understand the rationale behind a horrendous act.

A suspense novel often involves situations that are wide ranging—life on earth could be eradicated or a bomb could go off in an airport. On the other hand, **mysteries often are set in closed communities**—on an island, a small town, a college campus, a train, at a dinner party, etc. The confined community enables the protagonist to pursue the possible killer within a set range with a limited number of suspects.

Suspense novelist Lynette Eason has also mentioned other distinctions: An important element of a mystery is the **red herrings**—the suspects who look so likely…yet turn out not to be the perpetrator. In suspense, the protagonist is thrust into a **cycle of mistrust**. And, of course, if the protagonist trusts the wrong individual or group…well, that ratchets up the suspense. Mysteries' conclusions are **intellectually satisfying**. Suspense endings are **emotionally satisfying**.

As you ponder your current plot, test it out with these mystery/suspense traits. If your story lands squarely in the middle, well, I'd say you've written a bit of a muddle. You might want to rethink the way your novel unfolds and make sure it matches the genre for which you're aiming.

CHAPTER 13

Salable Writing: How Branding Helps You to Sell Your Work

By Janet Kobobel Grant

Interacting with writers at writing conferences provides me with insight into what conceptions—some accurate, some not—wannabe authors have about the industry. During a recent conference, individuals who sat at the table I hosted for dinner engaged in a lively discussion about what a brand is and how an author finds his or her brand.

Some of the strategy and rationale behind branding follow:

More than Commonality

Branding is more than finding the commonality in what you've written. A novelist at the table suggested her brand might be writing about teenage, female protagonists. Or maybe, she mused, kidnapping was her brand since that was an element in all of her stories. A certain type of character or using the same plot device does not form a brand. The teenage protagonist might suggest that part of the author's brand is writing Young Adult. Or kidnapping as a key plot element might mean the author naturally leans toward writing suspense. However, these are only the inklings of what might become a writer's brand, not a brand per se.

A Promise

Your brand is a promise to your reader that you will deliver a particular type of reading experience. Looking at authors whose books you enjoy can help you to understand on a deeper level what a writer's brand looks like.

For example, I appreciate Walter Mosley's writing. What expectations does the reader have when picking up one of his novels? His most popular series are the Easy Rawlins mysteries, which I know will deliver:

- A complex murder
- that takes place in LA in the 1950s
- with Easy Rawlins, an African American detective, trying to solve the mystery.
- Rawlins will encounter prejudice,
- and the story will depict life in an uneasy era for anyone with black skin.
- The characters will be depicted with depth,
- and the plot will be taut and disturbing.

Or let's look at a nonfiction writer, David McCullough. Certain elements of his writing immediately come to mind for me:

- An in-depth examination of a key historical person or event
- with intensive research,
- compelling writing, and
- fascinating, little-known details.

Both Mosley and McCullough have made—and kept—their promises about the type of reading experience they deliver with every one of their books. That experience is an expression of their brand.

Consequences of Brand Violation

Sometimes we figure out our brand when we violate it. Remember the novel John Grisham wrote that broke the boundaries of his brand? That would be *A Painted House,* which was published in 2010. Here's how Amazon's review of the book begins: "Ever since he published *The Firm* in 1991, John Grisham has remained the undisputed champ of the legal thriller. With *A Painted House*, however, he strikes out in a new direction. As the author is quick to note, this novel includes 'not a single lawyer, dead or alive,' and readers will search in vain for the kind of lowlife machinations that have been his stock-in-trade. Instead, Grisham has delivered a quieter, more contemplative story, set in rural Arkansas in 1952."

The book sold poorly (for a Grisham novel), and neither reviewer nor reader seemed able to muster any enthusiasm for it. *A Painted House* was fated to a sickly existence from the moment Grisham put his fingers to the keyboard to create the novel.

That outcome was predictable. Grisham violated the border he himself had created when he wrote legal thriller after legal thriller. (Note how the Amazon review so aptly describes what Grisham's brand is? See? Readers know what to expect.) Your brand is what people come to expect from you, and they don't like deviations.

"Is that fair?" you might ask.

I would argue that's the wrong question. Neither life nor art is fair. Grisham's success was based on delivering what readers had come to expect. To disappoint his readers was to choose not to have a successful book. He made the choice to step outside of his brand just once. Fair or not, he realized he was meant to write legal thrillers. (In 2016 he did write a fictionalized account of a potential medical breakthrough, but the book was published through Amazon, a digital edition only and is sixty-seven pages long—not even long enough to really qualify as a book.)

We feel the same way about our coffee machines, our top choice in chocolate, our favorite car make, and our #1 TV show. They all inherently have promised to deliver a type of experience. That is their brand.

When Consumers Brand

Sometimes consumers brand authors. While we would like to believe we have the right to brand ourselves, sometimes our readers brand us. They tell us what they like about what we deliver by buying a certain reading experience over and over again. If you write both fiction and nonfiction, and your fiction always outsells the nonfiction, your readers are branding you as a novelist. That's what they want from you. If you write suspense and historical novels, your readers will vote for which genre they want from you; they're unlikely to like both categories but will choose one over the other.

Branding is a label, but that label comes from consistently providing readers a certain type of experience—and it's one they want to have over and over again.

CHAPTER 14

Salable Writing: Is Branding a Four-Letter Word?

By Janet Kobobel Grant

Is branding a bad word? Or is it a word that can help you to break out of your current status (be that midlist or never-been-published)? My answer is...it is both a bad word and a good word.

Here's a recap of a conversation I once had during a writers conference (a different conference from the one mentioned in chapter 13). I was chatting with a woman who was unpublished but made her living as a marketer. She clearly was savvy about how to position her projects. But the problem was that she had written a historical romance and a nonfiction book that would appeal to a specific, broad, and easily located readership (books on parenting, dieting, or marriage are some examples that fit this description). Her question to me was: "Am I shooting myself in the foot by presenting to editors two very different types of writing?"

My answer: "I don't think so." Here's my reasoning: While some people are born branded and know who their audience is and how to reach it, most writers enter the world of publishing not sure which direction they should go. I advise those people to knock on all doors to see which one will open. It's a simple matter of The Open Door Policy. Once you land a contract, you can think about focusing on your branding.

Receiving a contract means you have put together a project that the publisher believes will find a ready audience and is tightly focused, and that the publisher perceives you have the means to help to publicize. It's a thumbs up on all fronts.

This particular conferee had presented her fiction and nonfiction projects to a variety of editors, and all of them requested to see the project pitched. Now, here's the smart action point that she took: She only presented one project to each editor rather than talking about both projects. She either knew that the editor acquired nonfiction only or, if an editor acquired both fiction and nonfiction, the writer would ask questions at the outset of the meeting to determine which project was most likely to interest the editor.

Why was that smart? If she had presented both, she would have looked as if she were flailing around to grab an editor's attention anyway she could. She would have looked unbranded. Editors and agents don't like unbranded because that often translates to unfocused.

But that's not always the case. This writer could, and I believe would, put all of her focus on whichever project ended up with a contract being offered. She had the know-how and the passion to pursue either. That's the crux of branding; it's a combo of walking through the door that opens and remaining true to your passion.

Two dangers exist in presenting more than one kind of branded project at a time:

- You could find both projects are happily received by different publishing companies. While that sounds great, two giant, golden-egg-laying geese have just landed in your lap. Now you have to write and market two projects, with two different audiences, at two different publishing houses, and figure out how to brand yourself while you're going in two directions. It's like starting two businesses simultaneously.
- You could distract yourself from purposefully branding yourself and becoming known as a certain type of writer to editors.

> Editors and agents have awfully good memories about what you've pitched them in the past. So if you pitch a nonfiction book to an editor one year and a fiction title next year, that editor is likely to remember...and to wonder if you understand the importance of branding.

I also would advise against having more than two categories you're working in because it is very difficult to write middle-grade fiction, adult fiction, and adult nonfiction. Well, it might not be hard to *write* in several genres, but it's only the extraordinary person who can effectively *market* in all of them. Most authors struggle with how to write fast and well, aggressively market their books, and develop a significant platform—all of which are requirements in today's competitive publishing world. But some authors take it a step too far and begin to choose their brand specifically on what they think they will sell, constantly shifting with the market in order to try and make more profit. And this is just not plausible.

To help you visualize what I'm propounding, Wendy writes in the next chapter about an author who, from the outside of the industry, looks like a Renaissance Man. But from the inside...well, that's a different story.

CHAPTER 15

Salable Writing: Will, the Renaissance Man, and Branding

By Wendy Lawton

Let me introduce you to a writer. We'll call him Will. He's good. Very good. He's also a fast writer. Everything interests him. No one could call Will a dilettante. In fact, if you knew Will, he might appear to you as very professional in his undertakings. Maybe he even appears as not simply an author, but a Renaissance Man. Editors like him, and he's worked with a number of them. With several articles under his belt, he sold a nonfiction book on parenting. He followed that up with one on how to run a successful business without middle management. Furthermore, he co-wrote a book with a diet doctor and then ghost-wrote a book for an NBA player.

But, as Will says, "That was then, and this is now." He's discovered fiction, and Will is passionate about the novel he's writing. It's an international espionage story, and his writing friends tell him it's good. He can't wait to finish it, but because of his financial situation, he's taking a break to work up a synopsis for a category romance so he can cash in on that hot market right now and try to get some impressive sales numbers to make the editors sit up and take notice. And though he's not serious about children's literature for the long haul, he has a new granddaughter so he wrote a series of picture books using a princess as the main character.

While Will looks good on the surface, he is in reality an agent's nightmare. Every book he writes creates a bigger mess. He isn't creating a brand for himself. Rather than pursuing writing in one category, he's fickle. He isn't creating an identity for himself as a writer.

His two nonfiction books were for two different audiences. If he gained readers with the first one, they certainly didn't follow him to the business book. Co-writing a modest diet book was a detour that would confuse any readers even further. We won't even talk about the celebrity ghostwritten project. And if his readers weren't confused enough before, now he's turned to fiction! Apparently his genre of choice is the international thriller, but before he even tries to get out there with it, he's chasing romance, something he thinks is an easy sell. (It's not. It's a highly specialized market that requires skill and sensibility.) Will and his plan are a mess.

When we talk about branding, many writers tune it out. Each time I bring up the B-word in a workshop, I invariably get someone who takes offense. "I refuse to be put in a box." Or, "I'm a generalist. Have pen, will write." Or even, "I want to be open to whatever I feel called to write." Many writers view the idea of specializing and branding as somehow dehumanizing.

Let me draw you a parallel. Let's say you have a thriving hardware store in a farming town. You work hard to stock all the things your customer needs. You maintain a list of your customers, and you let them know when the seed comes in for vegetable gardens and when hoses go on sale. You deliver, you keep in touch, and your customers are loyal because they know what they'll get at your store.

Now, let's say you grow tired of hardware. You took a pastry course in your spare time, and you decide to follow that passion. At first, you install a bakery case in the front of the hardware store. Most of your customers are confused. Farmers in overalls don't seem to want petit fours or designer cupcakes. Hardware sales drop 10 percent, but you're sure you'll make that up with the bakery. Baking takes up a good part of your time and, unfortunately, ordering hardware suffers. When old customers come in and can't find what they need, business drops off again.

You see the writing on the wall. You need the hardware business to fund your life while you try to get the bakery going. You move the bakery out of the hardware store and into its own building. Now it's not so confusing because you realized that you have two completely different businesses with two completely different customer bases. Trouble is, you don't have enough time, energy, or money to service both businesses.

So what does this have to do with writing?

If you've been writing historical suspense, that's your thriving hardware store, so to speak. Your readers know what to expect when they see your name on a book. If you've decided to try your hand at, say, contemporary women's fiction, your readers are going to be confused. Some will even be angry that they bought a book thinking it was one thing but then discovered that it was something different. You'll come to realize that the bulk of your readers will not follow you wherever your creativity takes you. They like a certain kind of book. They have expectations.

Will has never made much money as a writer, but he feels he's on his way. He takes pride in his ability to write anything and that publishing house personnel know him. Trouble is, he keeps watching other nonfiction writers who write book after book on variations of the same topic. They keep getting bigger and better speaking gigs, and they're making ten times the money he does. What's with that? And when it comes to novelists, he sees some of his friends getting bigger advances with each subsequent novel, adding to their readership with each newsletter, blog, and book club event.

Will doesn't understand that a writing career is exactly like building a business. You can't afford to change your customer base with each new product. If you don't build on the base you've already won, you'll be starting over each time. That's what Will is doing. Instead of giving his parenting readers another book, he dropped them and started over in the business world. Then he dropped both bases and moved to a health and wellness topic. And on he keeps going, expending energy and money to gain readers and then tossing them away.

So, if you want to branch out, realize you may have to continue to satisfy your old audience with what they expect. You need to start a new brand, maybe even with a pseudonym, to reduce confusion. You'll have to start all over and build your new readership from the ground up. Now you have two businesses, so to speak. The question is, do you have enough time to satisfy your core customer while building a new business? Can you write enough books to satisfy both audiences? Will there be enough money to promote to two different audiences?

When you first start writing, it's okay to experiment—to discover who you are as a writer. But just like in college, you can't remain undeclared forever. If you want a career—the kind that leaves a lasting legacy—you need to focus and build. When you finally do figure out who you are as a writer, then you can work on refining the qualities of a book that catch your audience's eye.

CHAPTER 16

Salable Writing: Finding the Right Title

By Janet Kobobel Grant

Once you've found an idea that really clicks with you and one that should do well in the marketplace, it behooves you to take some time to find the right title.

I often hear writers mumble that such an activity is a waste of time—the publisher will change the title anyway. Maybe. Maybe not—if you find the right title.

What does it matter? The first audience you will ever try to sell your project to isn't the reader; it's either an agent or a publisher. And, if you want your best chance possible, you need to come up with a razzle-dazzle title.

Here are a few questions to ask yourself about your title:

Does It Convey the Tone of the Book?

One of my clients wanted to title her novel *Conflict*. What genre do you think the novel is? It might surprise you that the plotline was about a playwright who was afraid of conflict—so much so she couldn't write conflict into her plays. The book was a romantic comedy. *Conflict* doesn't do it, does it? The book ended up being called *My Life as a Doormat (in*

Three Acts). That title much more effectively conveys the playful tone of the book. Be sure the title you choose is a reflection of what the reader will find inside the volume.

Does It Tell Enough to Intrigue the Potential Reader?

One author describes this as having both steak and sauce in a title. Offer both sizzle and substance in a title. For example, *Mennonite in a Little Black Dress: A Memoir of Going Home* was clever in that the cover showed a little black dress that was anything but Mennonite in style.

However, don't be so esoteric or literary that people can't figure out what your book is about (especially for nonfiction). Here are two obscure titles: Chuck Colson's *The God of Stones and Spiders* and George Otis, Jr.'s *Twilight Labyrinth.* Any guesses as to those books' content?

For nonfiction don't be afraid to have an intriguing title matched with a straightforward subtitle (thus offering both steak and sauce), such as *The Tipping Point: How Little Things Can Make a Big Difference.*

Does It Pinpoint Your Audience?

There's no mistaking the audience for these titles: *The Carb Lovers Diet: Eat What You Love, Get Slim for Life* and *What to Expect When You're Expecting.*

Does It Set Itself Apart from Other Titles for the Same Audience?

Positive Parenting: An Essential Guide does little to distinguish itself from the myriad of other parenting books. But here are some titles that clearly delineate what's unique about the content: *How to Talk So Kids Will Listen and Listen So Kids Will Talk; Calming Your Anxious Child: Words to Say and Things to Do;* and *Backtalk: Four Steps to Ending Rude Behavior in Your Kids.* As a parent, you would know which of those books fit what you were looking for. Yet each book is about talking to your child. Each has a clear, unique approach that is defined in the title.

Is It Memorable?

Author Julie Barnhill noted, "I think titles should be thought of much in the same manner as the names of children. You want something that rolls off the tongue." Can a potential buyer remember a title long enough to get to the bookstore to ask for it?

The Guernsey Literary Potato Peel Pie Society worked in a counter-intuitive way. Even individuals who have read the book can't remember the title! But you can recall key words that would enable a bookstore sales clerk to know immediately what you had in mind. "I'd like that potato pie novel." "Do you have that Guernsey Society book?" "I want that World War II novel no one can remember the name of."

Is It Clever?

Sometimes a clever title can cause a book browser to pick it up. *A Chicken's Guide to Talking Turkey to Your Kids about Sex* would stand out from all the other books about the same topic. *Bon Bon Voyage* and *Holy Guacamole* are two titles in Nancy Fairbank's culinary mysteries.

For Nonfiction: Does It Promise a Benefit Either in the Title or Subtitle?

The Motivation Switch: 77 Ways to Get Motivated, Stop Procrastination, and Achieve Success leaves no doubt as to the book's content and its benefit. A person seeking such a book would know immediately the answer to her quest was in her hands.

Other Hints to Make Your Title Stand Out:

- Use alliteration. Cozy mysteries seem especially prone to such titles. Here are few cozy titles: *Dying for Danish, Killer Cupcakes,* and *Cappuccinos, Cupcakes and a Corpse.* But alliteration can work on all manner of books. *The Complete Cooking for Two Cookbook,* for example, certainly keys into the concept of cooking.

- Use a line from the book, such as, *Are You There, God? It's Me, Margaret.*

A potential agent or publisher sees hundreds of titles every month (if not every week). We're not easily impressed as a result. Startle us with something so stellar we blink our sleepy eyes, perk up, and say, "Wha… what did you just say?" Honestly, we can be awakened from our stupor with exceptional titles.

Concepts, just like great titles can make us sit up and take notice too….

CHAPTER 17

Salable Writing: Elements That Make a Book High Concept

By Janet Kobobel Grant

If you had one to three sentences in which to convince someone to buy your book, what would you say? Your answer reveals whether your manuscript is high concept. **High concept is a term used in the film industry for an idea that's so simple you can describe it in one to three sentences.** Whether fiction or nonfiction, if your manuscript is high concept, it generally translates into a book contract and strong sales.

These elements are important for a book to be considered high concept:

Unique or Familiar with a Twist

High concept requires that the idea be unique or a twist on a familiar idea. Obviously, for a novel, you can't tell all the plot details in a sentence or two. Instead, you want to focus on what sets your story apart. For example, Rene Gutteridge's novel *Misery Loves Company* can be described this way: Unlike Stephen King's *Misery,* the tables are turned and a best-selling author kidnaps a fan to exact revenge.

Misery Loves Company is high concept because it's a twist on a story most of us are familiar with—and that original King novel, *Misery,* is high concept because it, too, was a twist on a familiar idea: a rabid fan wanting to get up-close-and-personal with a best-selling author.

For a nonfiction book, a potential reader might not get jazzed about a book recounting parenting challenges in today's plugged-in world. Been there, read that. But a book about a family that went unplugged every Sabbath for one year and spent that time together...not only is that idea engaging, but it is also high concept. The idea went from generic to unique.

Broad Appeal

The idea must be exotic without being weird, appealing to a broad audience. If you chose to write a novel about a chicken that wanted to occupy the farmer's body, that book probably wouldn't have broad appeal. A few other quirky thinkers might gravitate to the idea, but most readers would not find this a fascinating topic. It's unique but weird.

In nonfiction, if you wrote about a town that collected all the plastic bags in the community and piled them in the town's square, that's weird. What's the point? But if the town also made them into beautiful tote bags, donating the money to an environmentally-oriented nonprofit, that's sounding like an idea readers would want to check out.

Demonstrates Conflict or Problem

The high concept description contains the book's conflict or problem. For a novel, what problem is the protagonist trying to solve? If it's relevant and explains what's unique about the idea, you might also add what barriers make it difficult to solve. If the setting is an important part of the story, that should be included in the concept as well.

Gone with the Wind, for example, is a high concept book that I would describe this way: During the Civil War, Scarlett O'Hara, a cunning Southern woman, connives to find love but doesn't recognize it when she sees it. Instead, she spends most of her life pursuing someone who is unsuited to her.

Condensing such an immense work into two sentences leaves out vast swaths of details, but when boiled down to its essence, the concept can be communicated. I've provided the time period, just a glimpse of the setting, who the protagonist is, what (main) problem she's trying to solve and the major barriers she encounters.

For a nonfiction book, the problem it sets out to fix should be pretty apparent. If not, back to the drawing board with you!

All of these elements must be true of a manuscript for it to be high concept. If you can't check off from your list each of the above qualities, your idea isn't high concept.

The Importance of High Concept

Why is high concept even important? There are at least four reasons: First, **the idea of the book is sold over and over again**: to an agent, to an editor, to a publishing committee, to a bookstore buyer, to the reader, and to that reader's sphere of influence. If the book is hard to talk about, it's a lot harder to convince people to be interested. It's unlikely anyone in that string of individuals listed above will respond positively to this single sentence: "It's hard to describe, but it's great." Yawn.

Additionally, striving for a book that is high concept forces the writer to define what the core of the manuscript is about, and that definition will **keep the book from meandering**.

Another advantage is high concept **means the book is marketable**.

And finally, **high concept helps the writer to discover his/her voice.** The concept itself might help the writer to figure out the voice in which the book must be written.

When Rene decided to create a takeoff on Stephen King's book, she knew she would have to generate suspense and sustain it. As a matter of fact, when Rene first told me about this idea, her pitch to me contained *why* the fan was kidnapped. But that information is withheld in the book's back cover copy and in all publicity because giving away too much spoils the suspense. High concept is not only about what to put into your sentence (or two) but also what to leave out.

So far we've talked about whether your book idea is strong and if it's fresh. We've taken a look at the quality of your writing. We've evaluated if you've selected the right genre or category for your book, thought about your author brand, worked hard on the title, and can talk about your book's high concept in a couple of sentences.

Now that we have successfully navigated our way through refining your book idea, it's time to decide which publishing route is best for you.

PART TWO

The Inside Scoop on Deciding Between DIY and Traditional Publishing

CHAPTER 18

Self-Publishing vs. Traditional Publishing–Pros and Cons

By Janet Kobobel Grant

At writers conferences, I often hear statements that suggest conferees and even some faculty members view self-publishing as synonymous with a royalty-paying publisher. This, however, only leads to misinformation and confusion. Let's explore what self-publishing is, who benefits from it, and how it compares to traditional publishing (i.e., publishing with a publisher that pays royalties and does not ask the author to pay for any aspect of the book's production or marketing).

Traditional Publishing House Overview

- Project must make it over the hurdles of a publishing committee that includes sales and marketing staff before a contract is offered.
- An editor works with the author to refine the manuscript, possessing the power to declare the manuscript "unacceptable." This means the project isn't deemed publishable by the editor, so the rights are returned to the writer.

- Marketing personnel work as a team with the editorial and sales departments to create a cover they consider most likely to sell copies of the book.
- All of the sales staff (and there is a sales staff) are introduced to the project at a sales meeting and then sell the title to retailers and special markets both before the book is released and again after its release. Each title will appear in the publisher's catalog and on the publisher's website.
- A marketing and publicity budget is created for each title, with the publisher deciding what level of budget to apply to each book.
- The author receives an advance (payment to be deducted from royalties to provide the author with the financial resources to write the manuscript) and royalties, which are paid from copies sold.
- The publisher may have retained additional rights to the content and can therefore sell the rights to have the book published in other languages, as an e-book, as an audio book, etc.

Self-publishing Overview

- Some companies that offer services to provide a printed book have a few hurdles for a book to leap over, but most have none beyond the author having the funds to pay the publisher to create a book from the manuscript.
- Some self-publishing entities edit manuscripts, but since the writer is paying to have the book published, the manuscript won't be deemed unacceptable. It will be published.
- Marketing is available through some self-publishers, but the author will have to pay for the promotion.
- The covers of self-published books don't generally meet the level of design of a royalty-paying publisher's because the budget isn't large enough for such a cover. (Traditional publishers frequently pay $5,000 or more for the cover design.)
- No sales team exists in self-publishing. No presentations are made to Barnes & Noble, Wal-Mart Stores, or Costco. Yes,

the books might be available to those entities, but a sales rep doesn't present individual titles to each outlet.

- The author pays for everything: editing, designing of the cover, printing, and marketing. It's the other side of the coin from a traditional publisher in which the publisher undertakes all expenses connected to the production and sale of the book.
- Other methods of conveying the text—foreign languages, audio, etc.—will not be exercised by any self-publisher (even though some who call themselves independent publishers ask for those rights in their contract). Distribution in its many forms generally falls on the author's shoulders.

Traditional publishing and self-publishing are very different animals—rather like comparing a dog to a cat. And, just to complicate the possibilities, some publishers are a hybrid, a mix of traditional and self-publishing. I've found that almost all publishers refer to themselves as traditional publishers, even if they're hybrids. Buyer, beware.

As a writer surveys the landscape of traditional publishing vs. self-publishing vs. hybrid, which is the best choice? That depends....

When Should You Say Yes to Self-Publishing?

- You have the funds to pay for the publishing and marketing of your book.
- You have the ability to reach the book's audience. One of my clients self-published several books on Huntington's disease because she spoke regularly to audiences either afflicted with the ailment, caregivers of those afflicted, or medical staff. This built-in audience made it reasonable for her to self-publish since most traditional publishers wouldn't be able to reach that segment of readers, but she could. Another individual I know chose to self-publish his book on dieting because he figured he could make more for each copy sold than he could if he were paid a royalty. He was absolutely correct in his math, but he was incorrect in that he had no distribution channel to reach the overweight individuals in need of his dieting plan. In

retrospect, I'm sure he realizes he should have taken the mid-range advance a publisher was offering to pay him rather than shelling out the money to self-publish his book.

- You are willing and able to aggressively publicize your book. You are, after all, the publisher of the volume, so all the responsibilities—and rewards—of being a publisher default to you.
- You create a business plan rather than following the typical eyes-closed-to-reality approach. Costs are inherent in self-publishing; be prepared to confront the business side of the venture. The nice aspect of self-publishing is that you will make far more for each book sold than you can publishing via royalty-paying publishing. But, the vast majority of those who self-publish lose money rather than make it because they don't create a business plan and aren't realistic about the funds and focus it will take to find readers beyond friends and family.

Hybrid publishers, will take some of the responsibility off you for producing the book and selling it. But look each one over carefully to see if it can deliver what you need in a partner.

Now, if you're still on the fence, let's dig a bit deeper into the pluses and minuses of each approach to publishing.

CHAPTER 19

Digging into Traditional Publishing

By Janet Kobobel Grant

Traditional, royalty-paying publishing smooths an author's way through the publishing process. Such a publishing house offers a neat package to the writer that enables him or her to concentrate on creating a great manuscript.

Hey, I get that traditional publishing can seem like a fortress that's impossible to penetrate. Many publishers won't even accept a query from an un-agented writer, let alone offer to publish your work!

But publishers who make an investment of tens of thousands of dollars in your book bring a lot to the table. It's sort of like staying at a five-star hotel. Royalty-paying publishers have plenty of razzle-dazzle, at-your-service options to offer for no cost, including the following: an editor, who holds your feet to the fire and makes you create your very best work (along with a copyeditor and proofreader, who double- and triple-check your writing); a marketing staff, who have ideas to promote your work that would never have occurred to you; publicity people with connections in all the right places (You mean like Oprah?! Yup.); and a sales staff with working relationships with book buyers at all the major outlets and who are also paid to make regular calls on those buyers.

Okay, okay, I'm strutting the idealized version of a royalty-paying publisher. No, your book isn't necessarily going to be pitched to Oprah. No, your book won't necessarily get the Top of the Mark marketing budget. But my point is royalty-paying publishers have the wherewithal to provide all this and more. These publishers warehouse copies of your book, keep track of its inventory, send it out and send you money based on those sales, offer it to foreign language publishers, release your book in a variety of formats such as hardback, trade paper, mass market, and possibly a gift book or a workbook out of your material. These are the folks who have been creating books for a very long time. And, here's the really good news: They *want to pay you* to let them produce your book.

In talking with publishing house representatives, I'm regularly surprised at efforts they take to make their books successful that I wasn't aware of. Here's the inside scoop on what some publishers do.

One publishing house invites buyers from box stores (Costco, Wal-Mart, etc.), Barnes & Noble, and Books-a-Million to attend the publisher's sales meetings. The buyers are introduced to the new titles by editors and marketing folks at the same time the sales reps learn about the product. That creates great synergy, with key individuals in the publishing house hearing the buyers' responses and the buyers having the benefit of the editors' and marketing personnel's enthusiasm for a title, as well as for the author. If a series is in the mix, the editor can talk up how the future titles will build on the current offering. Such a relationship can generate pre-release excitement for a book from the individuals who decide how many copies the company will place in each store.

Another publisher sees its marketing job as finding new readers for an author; the author's job is to care for everyone who already has discovered the writer. That sort of task distribution helps both the publishing house and the author to understand what each should be doing. And each party can present ideas on how the other could maximize efforts. It's a give-and-take relationship, but certain duties (e.g., connecting via Facebook, Twitter, and blogging) fall on the author's shoulders, while other duties (e.g., creating blog tours, arranging interviews, making book memes, and sending out sales reps) fall to the publisher.

Using sales representatives as more than order takers is a key component for one of these publishing houses. The head of sales believes taking orders needs to be as streamlined as possible, so the rep is freed up to be a creative community builder. That means the reps are blogging, speaking at corporations, or even setting up retreats where readers can pay to join a group. And what the reps are saying through these venues isn't being channeled through them from headquarters; the salespeople's content isn't being monitored from on high. The reps are engaging not just with book buyers, but also with book *readers*—and working to build enthusiasm for books via word of mouth.

CHAPTER 20

Digging into Self-Publishing and Hybrid Publishing

By Janet Kobobel Grant

As I've mentioned in chapter 18, going the DIY route has merit for the person with the right project and the right mindset. These often are individuals who:

- Haven't found interest for their project with either an agent or a publishing house.
- Are willing to take on the job descriptions for everyone at the traditional publishing house from CEO on down. Perhaps, beyond actually writing the book, the project manager is the key to success since someone has to oversee the book moving from one phase of production to the next. (Keep in mind that several highly successful self-publishing authors have thrown in the towel and gone to a traditional publishing house out of sheer weariness from playing all these roles. It's not as easy as it sounds, especially if your book is selling like iced lemonade on a hot day.)
- Have the funds to create their own book and to market it. Having your book appear on Amazon can be done cheaply,

especially if you're willing and able to create your own cover and work with Createspace to format the book. But generally authors want to (and should) hire a content editor, a copy editor, a proofreader, and a graphic designer (or buy a ready-made cover). If all you care about is having a book to hand out to friends and family, you can cut the budget down to the nub. But if you want to attract readers who don't know you to buy your book and to look for your next book, you need to invest in making it a quality product both in its content and its look.

- Have an adventuresome spirit, willing to play with pricing and to study the results from your experimenting. What works to sell books today won't necessarily work tomorrow; it's an ever-fluctuating market.
- Are able to create an effective marketing/publicity campaign to get the word out about the book and to continue to market it.
- Are disenchanted with the chains that traditional publishing puts on an author. There's always someone telling you what will or won't be done to your book and for your book. These authors ask, "Why should I receive a small percentage of the sales revenue when it's my book!?" "Why shouldn't I have control over the cover?" "Why shouldn't I decide how much the book sells for?"

Some writers were born to self-publish; it's their happy place in the sun. Others see it as the perfect solution—until they dig into the reality of it. Still others have found a temperate approach works for them, publishing certain titles with traditional publishers and producing some titles on their own. Knowing your strengths and weaknesses and paying attention to them will guide you to the right spot for you.

But what happens if you dip your toes into self-publishing and then turn your attention to the traditional publishing world? How will agents, editors, and publishers view you?

CHAPTER 21

Publishing Perceptions

By Janet Kobobel Grant

Often when I'm on an agent panel at a writers conference, a conferee will ask, "If I self-publish, how will that be perceived by an agent or a royalty-paying publisher?" Here are my responses to the questions behind that question.

Does Self-Publishing Make the Book More Valuable?

Not really. Agents and traditional publishers understand that a self-published book was something a writer paid to have created. It only gains value if the writer was able to sell several thousand copies—like five thousand or more. Once you reach the ten thousand mark, that starts to gain real attention.

Does Self-Publishing Hurt My Chances in Finding an Agent?

Not really. To me, it's a neutral factor. Certainly I want to know that you have self-published and what the sales were. Self-publishing becomes an important factor only if you sold a ton of copies or have tied up the rights to the title so you aren't free to offer those rights to a publisher.

How Should I Present a Self-Published Book in My Bio?

It's important to specify that the book is self-published. I once heard an agent suggest to a panel's audience that no distinction exists between self-publishing and publishing by a traditional publisher, but that's simply not true. Just tell us the numbers you sold. And, if you offered one book for free to increase sales for other self-published books, mention how many were given away and what sort of sales surge you saw. All this helps the traditional publishing world to put your publishing experience into a context.

Here's how you would add this information to your bio: After you indicate that you've written a book (or books), be sure to mention the title, the category it falls into, that it is self-published or published by an independent publishing house, and the number of copies sold.

Ultimately, self-publishing has little effect on your traditional publishing future—unless your success shows that:

- An audience exists for your work.
- A larger audience awaits your book (in other words, you haven't already sold copies to most of the people who would want to buy them).
- You have marketing skills and a growing e-mail list, Twitter followers, Facebook friends, etc., that can be applied to projects published by a traditional publisher.

For the most part, self-publishing a book or books is neutral—or positive, if you did it successfully. There are, however, exceptions—when the writer didn't do it well.

CHAPTER 22

Crossing Over from Self-Publishing to Traditional

By Wendy Lawton

First of all, let me clear up a misunderstanding: Some writers contact an agent with a self-published project and ask if we can help them market it. That request grows out of confusion as to what we do. We may help our clients to navigate different marketing options. We may even help to brainstorm marketing initiatives for our clients, but when authors come to us, they should be seeking literary representation, not book marketing. If self-pubbed authors want help getting the word out about their books, they need to look for a book marketing firm.

Here's the problem with the authors seriously seeking literary representation: If you are coming to me to represent a book that is already published, I can only assume the DIY process was a failure. If it's going gangbusters, why would you want to pay me a percentage of your royalties? Even if I loved a self-published book, the first question I'm going to ask is, "How many copies have been sold?" And I'm going to need to see documentation of that. Remember, when we are considering taking on a new client, we are not only assessing the work but also analyzing which publishers will be interested. If you are selling like the almost mythic

Amanda Hocking, then a publisher will jump at the chance to re-publish the book. If you sold three or four thousand e-books in the first year at $3.99 per book, then not so much.

Several factors work against you if you self-publish and then seek an agent and traditional publisher:

- You've demonstrated the vigor of your own platform. It's now quantifiable. That can be a good thing or a bad thing depending on how vigorously the book sold.
- Building a significant literary career takes perseverance. Some agents and publishers view the self-published author as one who lacks the patience to build slowly and strategically.
- When you make a choice to go it alone, some professionals could see it as a maverick attitude. Does it denigrate what a whole team brings to the process?

All that said, some books are meant to be self-published, which Janet explores in Chapters 18, 20 and 21. These books appeal to the author's own, well-known niche: books written by speakers and marketed to their audiences and books created for an event or company.

Be aware of these potential pitfalls when you approach a literary agency after self-publishing. Be sure to portray your goals clearly after looking over the agency's services. Furthermore, be prepared to answer questions like the ones above and, even more, prepared to make a case as to why the agent should choose to represent your book.

CHAPTER 23

Before You Take the DIY, Independent Publishing Plunge

By Janet Kobobel Grant

As DIY publishing and independent publishing continue to develop, I'm seeing several common mistakes that writers make. Here's a brief list of suggestions to consider before you launch your sailboat into those waters.

- **Don't panic.** I've found that many authors feel pressure to publish out-of-print titles, manuscripts tucked away in old files, blogging posts—really, anything at hand. Authors seem to believe that if they don't get these works out there now, they are lagging behind, not keeping up with the times, and ultimately causing the demise of their careers. Actually, the opposite could well be true. To publish books just because you can but without creating a thoughtful plan as to what you're publishing, when you're publishing it, and why you're publishing it, is to lead to a potentially lost opportunity later on. Self-publishing isn't going to go away; as a writer, you want to launch into this venture purposefully rather than randomly. Panic is seldom a smart motivator.

- **Don't necessarily go with the first independent publisher you connect with.** New publishers are sprouting up every day. As in traditional publishing, each has its strengths and weaknesses. Some will exist long-term; others are fly-by-night.
- **Don't forget to read the contract.** I've seen several independent publishing contracts, and they're all over the place. No templates exist. Some are draconian; others quite fair. You, of course, know what the royalties are, but do you also know how to get your rights back if this publisher doesn't meet its commitments or if the publisher goes belly up? There are many factors to understand before signing.
- **Involve your agent.** If you're fortunate enough to have an agent, please take advantage of your agent's expertise. I'm befuddled as to why an author would not include his or her agent in this extremely important part of a writing career. Some of my clients plunged ahead without me but then asked me to step in to rescue them when it all went terribly wrong.
- **Don't choose to believe that because you can, you should.** I'm rounding the corner to come back to the idea of being intentional. One of my clients received requests from a couple of book clubs for an out-of-print book and decided it was an indication of a significant readership just awaiting that now out-of-print book. Really? I'd encourage you to dig deeper into just how big that demand is. And if the demand is fledgling, do you have the resources to build on it through marketing, publicity, strong mailing list, major following in social media, etc.? Just because you can bring your books back to life, doesn't mean you should.
- **Know your readership.** Do your readers own e-readers? Smart phones? Shelves and shelves of physical books? How do they want your books delivered to them? Do they read only fiction

on an e-reader? If you don't know what your readers want, how do you know what to give them?

If you avoid these mistakes, DIY book publishing can be a great route to take. Just like all publishing methods, it does have its downsides, especially if you rush through the process; however, taking time to carefully understand what you're doing can set you on the right track.

PART THREE

The Inside Scoop on Presenting Your Idea to an Agent

CHAPTER 24

I Don't Need No Stinkin' Agent

By Wendy Lawton

If you hope for a significant writing career, one of the best things you can do is to amass an ace team. That would include an agent, maybe a publicity or social media consultant, a critique team, some fellow writers to help brainstorm, a few beta readers, and the start of a group of influencers. Yup, I included agent.

Can you go it alone in this day and age? Sure, especially if you aren't planning to publish traditionally. And it's possible to agent yourself even if you're going to publish traditionally. But why would someone want to? I'm an experienced agent, but when I write, do I represent myself? Are you kidding? If I did, I would have a fool for a client. After all, even the Lone Ranger had Tonto and Silver.

Despite what you may have heard from a few of the self-proclaimed DIY publishing gurus, if you want to build a lasting career, you will eventually need an agent on your team. Agents add real value to an author's team. Show me a *New York Times* mega-best-selling author who does not have an agent. It doesn't matter that they could sell their books to any publisher themselves if they chose to do so. These savvy authors understand that it's a complicated world, and they are smart enough to surround themselves with as many experts as they can.

For those of you who may be skeptical, let me mention a few things an agent does:

- **An agent is your worrier-in-chief.** Because our experience spans many publishers and many careers, we are the ones who see patterns. Agents know where and when the bumps are likely to occur.
- **An agent is your air traffic controller.** Publishing is becoming ever more complex. Your agent is going to be the one to safely land all the planes that are circling (new releases, self-published books, re-releases, etc.). We're seeing all kinds of collisions on the publishing runway these days. Some of these can be fatal to a career.
- **An agent offers industry-wide perspective.** Writers know what's happening anecdotally, which is less than reliable. Publishers know what's happening in their company. Agents are the ones who have an idea of what's happening across the board. We see royalty statements from all the publishers. The information is proprietary, and we never share, but we have a perspective unique in this industry.
- **An agent handles many of the time-consuming details so the author is free to create.** This is one of the best benefits. Yes, you might be able to do it all, but is that the best use of your time?
- **An agent is a specialist in publishing contracts.** You often hear people say that a writer could simply hire an attorney to look at publishing contracts. We smile. Publishers groan. An attorney who is not familiar with publishing contracts would have to spend hours getting up to speed. They would question every clause, not understanding the concepts. And did I mention that their confusion is all on your dime? However, agents have seen so many contracts that we can usually figure out quickly what needs to be adjusted.

  In the end, the contract we have negotiated with the publisher is usually far different from the boilerplate version the publisher's attorney has created. A literary agency starts out negotiations for you using a template of the publisher's contract that the agency has been working to improve every time the agency has sold a project to the publisher. Remember: Every clause in the publisher's contract was written to the publisher's advantage; that's the language you'll find in the boilerplate. While the agency will not have managed to reverse all that to the author's favor, significant progress will have been made. And we've used the leverage of our best-selling authors to get there. Then you get to take advantage of years of our work.

- **An agent is the bad cop that allows the author to be a good cop.** Without an agent, you are the one who must deal with all the troubles that arise. And trouble always arises. We, on the other hand, have long-term relationships with editors, publishers, etc. that can be leveraged to fix problems and craft win-win situations. And when push comes to shove, we are okay with being the bad guys, which leaves your publishing relationships untarnished.
- **An agent offers a collaborative community.** Not all agents gather their clients together in a tribe, but when it happens, it is invaluable.
- **An agent reads widely in the industry, staying on top of things to keep her clients apprised.** Part of our job is to stay on top of trends and industry issues. We read intentionally and widely. The agents within an agency generally have regular meetings to discuss what they are reading and hearing.
- **A good agent rarely costs the client anything.** Some authors cite the commission we take as a reason to sidestep having an agent, but we usually negotiate a deal with the publisher that more than compensates for our cost. And we don't get a cent until you make money. (We're paid a commission from your earnings.)

These are stats you'll never see, but if you could compare well-agented writers against un-agented writers . . . well, 'nuff said.

CHAPTER 25

Two Things an Agent Is Not

By Janet Kobobel Grant

Writers are often unclear about what an agent actually does. Conversations with writers over the years have helped me to understand that would-be or even current clients can misconstrue an agent's role in two ways.

An Agent Is Not a Magic Wand

An established author contacted me about representing him. As we discussed the current state of his career, I discovered:

- He never had an agent because he never saw the utility of that relationship.
- He had negotiated bad contracts and bad deals for himself.
- He had moved to a new publisher despite the top billing his old publisher had maintained for him.
- The new publisher wasn't promoting his most recent release, and his sales numbers were in serious decline.

The author was thinking that maybe an agent could get him some marketing bucks for his release and get him out of his multi-book contract. I concluded that said author's career called for triage. Yet the author had no idea how imperiled he was. However, one thing he thought he knew: An agent could wave a magic wand and make it all better.

Nope. Ain't going to happen.

Now, we agents can pull rabbits out of the hat...sometimes. We can rescue careers...sometimes. But still, we offer no guarantees that we can fix what has gone dreadfully wrong and sometimes has taken years to get as bad as it is. We also can't resolve problems with a book as it is being produced if the author doesn't tell us things aren't going well.

An Agent Is Not a Life Preserver Used Only in Case of Emergency

A friend recently connected me with an author who had written a manuscript that had best-seller written all over it. But the writer was new to publishing and confused about why she needed an agent. She had, in fact, contacted a publishing house that was wooing her toward a book contract. The author riddled me with questions about what an agent could do for her, and I launched into a round of mini-workshops on what agents do that go way beyond finding a publishing home for a project. I explained that I was pretty certain several publishers would be interested in her project, and that it would be in her best interests to give me a chance to show the project around.

But the writer liked how excited the publishing house she had contacted was. She couldn't see that she was short-changing herself by not signing with an agent and giving that person free rein to do what agents know how to do: elicit significant interest from a number of publishers and choose the house that has the most enthusiasm for and willingness to invest in a project.

Two days after the writer and I went our separate ways, I received a panicked email saying the publishing house she was so sure was perfect for her had turned down the project. I suspect that happened because she insisted that the book be released in three months, which I had explained to her was seriously off-putting to publishers.

"Take my project to other publishers," she wrote in her succinct email.

I think she pictured me as a life preserver, and she had just realized she was in a storm-tossed sea.

Once again: Ain't going to happen.

She already had shown herself incapable of trusting me to take care of her and her project. If I chose to represent her and started to work on her behalf, I was pretty sure she would be chaotic enough to take over the process from me, muddying the waters with unrealistic expectations. I loved her project, but she was impossible to work with. I couldn't be her life preserver.

The two takeaways I would suggest from these stories are:

- Realize your agent can only work with what you give him or her. If you don't have a stunning project, if you aren't building your platform, or if you don't want to concentrate on writing manuscripts that build a brand, you are asking your agent to be a magic wand.
- Understand that a writer's unrealistic expectations about the size of an advance, the best way to move his or her career forward, or what a publisher can or should do for a project put the agent in the role of a life preserver—and a preserver that is called into play only when it's an emergency. And there will be an emergency, probably more than one. Agents are useful for a number of reasons, but placing unrealistic expectations on them is not beneficial to either one of you.

CHAPTER 26

Why Do Agents Visit Publishing Houses?

By Janet Kobobel Grant

One of the most important things an agent does for his or her clients is to find a publishing house for their books. To do so, an agent must build relationships with many different houses. Oftentimes that's done through traveling to the houses. What exactly happens when the agent is there?

Client Meetings

Writing careers are complex animals, and sometimes the best way to bring an author and a publisher together as a team is to put them physically together in the same room. The meetings might be to introduce an author to the entire publishing team, either because the publishing house is very interested in a project and wants to meet the author or because the author has just signed a significant contract with the publishing house. Everyone has a lot at stake in these relationships, and nothing helps to kick off the team spirit like brainstorming on marketing and publicity ideas and hearing the author's heart for the project in person.

Dialoguing with the house about what an author's brand should look like on the cover and collateral material like marketing and publicity, is very important for an author's career. So is how an established author's brand can be updated yet remain true to the initial look, and how to transfer that same look to new product. The plan is to agree about how to move forward with the design of all these elements. There's nothing like sitting down at a conference table to make the way forward clear to everyone. Significant synergy can occur as one group's ideas spark ideas for everyone.

Project and Business Issues

An agent can decide to visit a publishing house sans author if a face-to-face meeting hasn't occurred naturally via a book convention or writers conference. Relationships deepen and the dynamics of what each party needs from that relationship unfold during these meetings. Relationships are an important part of the partnership that publishing entails. When an agent understands the publisher's needs (in terms of contractual issues, financial issues, and types of projects sought) and the publisher understands the author's needs, the likelihood of making a good match of author to publisher or satisfactorily negotiating contractual terms is greater.

Furthermore, sitting down with an editor or an editorial team and having those individuals showcase which of their recent releases have done well and which were disappointing is enlightening. I remember a trip in which an acquisitions editor showed me a title a lot like one a client of mine wanted to write. The editor explained that it never took off, despite the author's sizable blog audience. The publishing team had determined that the author was offering the same sort of material in a book form as she had created on her blog. Why should her readers buy what they were receiving for free? I realized my client was stepping onto that same path. When I returned to the office, the author and I discussed ways to make her book's offerings unique from her blog content. It was a lesson I still tell my clients so they don't make the same misstep that unfortunate author did.

Project Pitches

Pitching projects to an editorial team is educational, too. A lot of discussion takes place in the face-to-face conversations as editors give agents feedback, such as, "My sister was looking at the list I've built and pointed out that I'm tending toward publishing dark novels. So, yes, I do want to see this romantic comedy," or, "I think I've overbought in romantic suspense, so even though this idea sounds great, I'm going to pass," and even, "I've met [insert author's name here] at a writers conference and had the best conversation with him. Yes, I'd like to look at his project."

Intervention

Lastly, if an author-publishing relationship isn't going well, we step in. If communication is strained between an author and a publishing executive—or publishing team—sometimes that will call for a visit to the publishing house. Thankfully, these are less common.

Regardless the reason I am at the house, I always leave these meetings with plenty of notes about what a particular publishing house is looking for right now—not a few months ago when we talked last—but now.

CHAPTER 27

How to Approach an Agent: The Rules

By Wendy Lawton

Agents are approached by authors in any stage of their careers—from unpublished to best-seller status. But the following tips should help you to know how to present your book and maintain an efficient relationship regardless what stage your career is in.

How Do You Find an Agent?

First, when you consider what agents to submit your work to, ask yourself what kind of culture you want to be a part of. There is no one right answer. Some writers long to be with an agency that is considered a shark. Conversely, others want to be in an agency that takes a longer view of a writer's career.

Here are some of the questions you can ask an agent to help you determine the culture of an agency:

- Do you see your workplace as hierarchical, collegial, or highly individualistic?
- When the staff has meetings, how is information dispensed: give-and-take manner, conversational approach, key sources (especially management) dispensing information from key

sources (especially management), or attendees' reports on results from assigned work?
- How do you involve authors in decisions on their projects, such as titles, covers, and marketing?
- In what ways do you plan with authors to help them to grow their careers?

Next, once you've determined what type of agency is right for you, instead of sending out a generalized "Dear Agent" email, select the agents with whom you'd most enjoy working. When you query the agent, do it by name and explain what made you choose him or her. Far too often, we see queries that are scatter-gunned out there, sometimes by the author, but way too often by a supposed agent-find service. One quick look tells us that the writer has no idea what we do or who we are. If, at this honeymoon stage, writers can't invest in due diligence and target their queries, why would we think they would be able to study the market and target their readers? Yes, it takes a huge investment of time. And yes, the process is slow and tortuous, but this is nothing compared to the next steps. Being a working writer is not for the faint of heart.

Research the Agency

That being said, know as much as you can about the agent before approaching him or her. I'd love to see a study done comparing the effectiveness of targeted queries vs. the shotgun approach. I'm guessing that no matter how wide the shotgun scatter, the targeted, individual query receives far better results.

These days, it's so easy to research agents. Their websites spell out their distinctions, their likes and dislikes, and highlight many of their projects and clients. Follow the agency guidelines for contact information and protocol, which can usually be found on the agency website. Never call. There's nothing an agent can tell about your writing from a phone call. The reason agents ask you to query or propose is that it provides a window into your skill as a writer.

You can often ignore the contact rules if you're a successfully published author looking to make a change, if you've been referred by one of the agent's clients, or if you've met the agent in person and he or she has given you permission to skip the query step. (We'll talk about queries in upcoming chapters.)

What to Prepare

So, after all this, what do you actually show to an agent? You don't always have to present a complete manuscript. However, it depends on your publishing history.

- If you are writing a nonfiction book and have some writing experience, a finished manuscript is usually unnecessary. Most nonfiction books are sold based on the complete proposal—including a chapter-by-chapter summary and three chapters.
- If you are a published author, chances are the agent you've pinpointed will read your published work to decide. All she'll need to see from you is your proposal—including synopsis and about fifty pages.
- If you are a much-published novelist, you probably won't even need your next book synopsis—the agent will already be familiar with your work. Just pick up the phone.
- If you are a debut novelist, you'll need to have the proposal, including synopsis and the complete manuscript.

Also, you don't need to have your book professionally edited beforehand. Okay, let me soften that a bit. It depends on how much the editor does. An agent needs to judge your work and your voice. Unless you and the professional editor come as a package deal for every future project, how can the agent tell which part is you and which part is the editor? It's like having your mom help with your homework.

That's not to say you shouldn't have other eyes look at your manuscript. Critique groups are great for pointing out gaps in your story or illogical jumps in your reasoning. The difference is, they usually don't fix it. Rather, you solve the problems yourself.

But what about copy editing for spelling and grammar? Nothing is inherently wrong with this since the manuscript needs to be nearly perfect. But, if you're going to be a writer, isn't this one of those skills you need to attain yourself?

Communication Protocol

Lastly, here are some basic tips on how to communicate with your new agent efficiently:

- While making the decision to sign with an agent, you should have learned that agent's style. It doesn't hurt to ask for specifics at any time. Appropriate questions include the following: How often will we talk? How do you like to be contacted, by phone or email? How long can I expect to wait to have a question answered?
- Be sure to communicate in the preferred medium for your agent. He or she probably has a system for dealing with and archiving communication. For example, I primarily use e-mail. When a client or potential client contacts me via Twitter or Facebook, his or her note runs the risk of getting missed or misfiled.
- Make sure your agent is in the loop with any important discussions at your publishing house.
- As for the generic rules? Just follow rules of etiquette. Common sense and an attitude of graciousness and gentility will work in a pinch.

Here's the good part of all this extra work: Once, you've found your agent, she's made the sale, and you are connecting with your readers, I'm guessing you'll be the first to raise your hand and confess that it's worth the pain.

CHAPTER 28

When to Submit to an Agent

By Wendy Lawton

Back in the days when I was writing and submitting my work, hoping to catch the interest of an agent or editor, I would spend hours strategizing the perfect time for my query or proposal to land on their desks. Now I'm letting you in on my little secret and showing you my cheat sheet to save you hours of analysis.

A few of the **worst** times for your work to appear:

- The weeks just prior to a major trade show like Book Expo, which is held in May
- The weeks just after a major trade show
- The week before a writers conference at which the agent or editor is giving a presentation
- The week after a writers conference
- Three or four weeks after a writers conference when all the requested manuscripts begin to come in and bury your submission
- The week before the editor's or agent's vacation
- The week before or after a three-day weekend
- Thanksgiving week

- The week before Christmas
- The week after Christmas
- The week or two following NANOWRIMO

How about the **best** of times?

- The day your target agent or editor finally cleaned out his inbox and answered all his queries
- The day your agent or editor decided he or she is looking for the exact book you've written
- The first week of the year unless, like two of our Books & Such agents, your recipient is attending a New Year's conference
- The first week in September (another new year of sorts), as long as the recipient has no major writing conferences to attend
- In one of the ho-hum months during which nothing much is happening, such as the summer doldrums

Hopefully you've already guessed this is written with tongue-planted-firmly-in-cheek. There is no way, short of being a stalker, you can pick the perfect time for your query or proposal to land on the agent's or editor's desk. All my strategizing in the day was probably a huge waste of energy!

Good timing is one strategy to increase your chance of catching an agent's eye…but what if I told you there were other ways? Ways that didn't use the agent's crowded front door?

CHAPTER 29

The Backdoor to Literary Representation

By Wendy Lawton

So...you need a literary agent. You know you have a knock-'em-dead manuscript, but now you have to find an agent to represent you.

You've done everything right. You've gone to the agency website to see what it wants and how to submit the material. You've sent the query according to exact agency specifications. You don't even think of sending an attachment without an invitation. You wait and you wait and you wait.

So what's the problem? Agents are inundated with good queries, proposals, and manuscripts. In fact, a backlog of outstanding potential sits in the agent's inbox. What's a writer to do? Shhh...come closer and I'll let you in on a secret.

That's the front-door route to literary representation. But where there's a front door, there's often a backdoor that we use informally.

When I looked at my client list, I found six backdoor routes. It was eye-opening. *Only 4 percent of my clients came to me through a query.* Most came through the backdoor.

Let me break that statistic down even further:

- **42 percent of my clients met me at a writers conference**. I may not have signed them the first time we met, but as I got to know them, I knew I wanted to be on their team. A writers conference is my favorite way to meet new writers because I can observe them in a professional setting, see how they interact with people, and talk with them at length.

- **20 percent of my clients came via a client referral**. When one of my clients asks me to look at a writer's work, that request takes precedence. My clients know me, and they know good writing. You have to keep getting to know other writers and mention you are seeking representation. If they know you and know your work, they'll offer an introduction if it's appropriate.
- **16 percent of my clients I met through writing groups, online writing forums, or through our blog community**. I have been in writing groups online for more than fifteen years and have met a lot of writers that way. I've also been in local writing groups. When we see a name we recognize, it goes to the top of the pile. It's just natural.
- **8 percent of my clients were brought to me by editors**. Yes, some writers may already be publishing through a traditional publisher, but a good editor knows authors need an agent to help them to build a career for the long haul. We love it when a respected editor asks us if we'll consider one of their authors. It's a compliment.
- **8 percent of my client list came from my actively seeking them out**. It's true. We sometimes see an author we're crazy about, and if they aren't represented yet, we actively woo that person to come join us. Or sometimes we find a blogger whose work is the talk of the town, and we seek them for a book (yes, we stalk authors).
- **2 percent of my clients came from a contest win**. When an agent judges a writing contest, he or she is looking hard for that take-my-breath-away manuscript.

Of course, these stats are different for every agent, even within our own agency. One of our agents actively mines the query file to find her golden projects. Another of our agents proactively seeks rising voices. But this gives you an inside look. There's always the formal front entrance, but come around back, and you may find a wider welcome mat.

So those are the stats, but let me talk a little bit more about using these front door and backdoor strategies. We also call them workarounds.

CHAPTER 30

Workarounds to Literary Representation

By Wendy Lawton

The Oxford English Dictionary gives the following definition of a *work-around*: "A (usually temporary or makeshift) means of bypassing or resolving a technical difficulty when a system, procedure, or mechanism fails to work; a method of overcoming a performance issue or limitation in a program. Now also more generally: a means of avoiding or resolving a problem when the usual or most obvious solution is not feasible, possible, or available."

When encountering computer problems, I avoid workarounds. I say, work through the problem to keep everything humming. But how many times have we acknowledged that the system for finding your agent is seriously flawed? As our definition says, it is a "technical difficulty when a system…fails to work."

Could it call for a workaround?

I'm going to offer four different ways to get around the faceless, flawed agent query system. The system would work fine if there were ample slots for every good writer, but there aren't. It's more like succeeding in Hollywood–a combination of who you know, the level of your talent, the current opportunities, the climate for your type of talent, and just plain being in the right place at the right time.

Let me break down the workaround specifics:

Problem: Catching the attention of an agent and getting him or her to ask for a proposal or manuscript.

Traditional Solution: Write a smashing query letter, send it to multiple agents, and hold your breath.

Workaround: One way around the oh-so-slow agent query is to come to that agent with a referral from one of his clients. Our clients become our best screeners. When I get a referral from a trusted client, I try to drop everything and give the submission my full attention.

Here's the rub: You cannot put that writer on the spot by asking for a referral. And you cannot approach a stranger to do this. If the client is not familiar with you and your writing, he could never put his reputation on the line to refer you. His referral capital, so to speak, is only valuable if he has a good eye and the ability to offer a great possibility to the agent.

So, if you can't ask directly and you can't enlist strangers, how in the world do you go about getting a referral? It has to do with investing in other writers over a long period of time. When you first start writing, you need to join the community of writers online. You begin to identify writers you enjoy. You give them Amazon reviews. You write on their Facebook pages. You retweet their tweets. You attend their events and book signings. You join a local critique group of writers who are a step or two ahead of you.

As you get to know writers and invest in them, let them reciprocate. Let them read some of your work and get to know you. If the two of you click and the relationship is reciprocal, it can turn into friendship. And it definitely doesn't hurt to let your friends know you are seeking referrals at some point. Let them tell you when they think you are ready.

You can tell this isn't something you decide you need and just set out to make happen. You need to honestly connect with the community of writers from the very beginning. Your friends will help you work around some of these odds. It's no surprise that so many published authors are friends–they've been helping each other for years.

Problem: Catching the attention of an agent and getting him to ask for a proposal or manuscript.

Traditional Solution: Write a smashing query letter, send it to multiple agents and hold your breath.

Workaround: This one is simple. Enter writing contests in which your target agent or editor is a judge. Many contests ask professionals to judge the final round, and we are delighted to do so because by the time we receive the manuscripts, they have gone through a serious winnowing process. Others have done the work for us, and we get to read the cream of the crop. When we read those entries and find one we love, once the judging is done, we ask the contest coordinator for that person's contact info.

So where do you find the contests? Check out the list in the back of the *Writers Market* and online at such sites as www.winningwriter.

Problem: Catching the attention of an agent and getting him to ask for a proposal or manuscript.

Traditional Solution: Write a smashing query letter, send it to multiple agents, and hold your breath.

Workaround: Rather than send an anonymous query letter, you can send a query that comes from a very familiar name. How? By interacting with your target agent online. When readers comment on our blogs, befriend us on Facebook, or retweet our tweets, we can't help but remember those names. Each time you leave your name, you are leaving a positive brand impression, so to speak. The more positive brand impressions, the more memorable you'll be.

Many writers wonder if social networking works. If you are personable, helpful and regular, your name is getting out there. And name recognition is the antidote to being anonymous. As a writer seeking representation, make sure you use your full name—the same way it would come to an agent with a query. It's just one more way of becoming unforgettable.

I hope these workarounds help you to see that for every front-door approach there is no end of creative entrances to get in the door. No matter which route you take, the important thing is to be natural and winsome. Being pushy or insistent does not help you build a relationship with an agent, is even more detrimental in a face-to-face contact, and even more so when you are on a first-name basis with that person.

CHAPTER 31

What Does It Mean When an Agent Responds to My E-mailed Query?

By Wendy Lawton

A couple of weeks ago, one of my clients wrote to me the following:

As I've observed and visited with many unpublished authors who attend conferences, I find that the trend increasingly leans toward an editor and/or agent asking them to send their manuscripts or additional work for review. No matter what else they may be told during that appointment, they hear NOTHING but the fact that someone has asked for their manuscript, and they believe they are now going to be published.

Weeks, months, and sometimes more than a year will pass, and they hear nothing. They don't know whether to send to someone else, "bother" the agent/editor they've sent it to for they fear that will anger them, or continue to hope and believe it's going to all happen in time.

During my earlier years at conferences, editors and agents frequently sat people down and said, "You show some promise, but you need more work." Or, "Your writing skills aren't quite up to snuff—how about considering some additional classes and mentoring?" Anyway, you get the idea—they took it as their responsibility to tell these hopeful authors the truth. And, believe me, I know that's a hard thing to say to someone. But is it not better to speak the truth in love than to let these folks sit for months on end thinking they've just been given a golden ticket?

That is a tough indictment but is nonetheless valid. Therefore, I've decided to try to decode some of these unspoken agent signals. However, let me first offer a disclaimer: These observations are based largely on my own practices and those I've observed from the many agents I know and admire. But each agent is different (just like writers) and has different strengths and weaknesses. When it comes to your experience with agents, YMMV (your mileage may vary).

So what does it really mean when you've emailed a query to an agent—or mailed it, depending on the agent's stated preference—and you get a response that says "send the proposal," or even "send the whole manuscript"?

Here's how I would decode that request: The agent is sincerely interested, based on your query. When an agent works through his or her queries, he has set time aside to focus on finding excellence and is in peak analytic mode. He doesn't do this when he is stressed, tired, or overwhelmed—which is why it sometimes takes a while to hear back. So if you receive a request for further material, consider it a sign of solid interest.

Many agencies, like Books & Such, do not reply if uninterested. These agencies usually give a specific timeframe. "If you don't hear back from us after [set amount of time], you'll know we are not interested." Books & Such, for one, makes sure to honor the stated date. *All* queries are read, so if the time frame passes without word, the writer knows.

Why do agencies do this? Because of the sheer volume of queries. It is not possible to get back to everyone who queries. Few of us have sufficient staff to accomplish that task, even if we only used a form response that would tell the writer nothing anyway.

Writers often bemoan the lack of feedback. "How do we know why our query didn't interest you if we never get any feedback?" If you've been in this industry—reading blogs and attending conferences—you already know the answer. It's a limited resource issue—agents simply do not have the time or staff to give feedback. Those of us who love to interact and mentor hate that aspect of this system, but it's a reality.

Besides that, we've been trained by the few bad apples who don't understand the realities. In our early years as agents, many of us tried to give a little feedback, which invariably opened a stream of dialogue—either vitriolic anger, prolonged argument, or request for clarification. We're fast learners. It didn't take long to realize it was safer to refrain from any specific comment.

So what does it mean if you don't hear back? It could mean the agent is saying:

- "Scary! Really scary. Make sure to block sender."
- "Writing doesn't seem to be quite there yet."
- "Umm, nope. I don't think so."
- "Good idea. If only my list weren't so full."
- "Good idea, but, unfortunately, the writer doesn't have the platform to interest publishers."
- "Good idea, but I have [client's name], who is already filling this slot."
- "Good idea, but not right now. Sadly, the market's not there at this time."
- "Interesting writer, but not a fresh idea. I've seen this same idea/plot too many times recently."

I know, I know. That doesn't help you decode a no or a nonresponse. You'll have to look for other clues. But at least you now know the spectrum of reasons you didn't hear back.

Next, I'll address what it means when an agent begins to informally communicate with you, which addresses some of those clues above. In that context, I'll circle back to answer my client's initial concern when we consider what it means when an agent requests your proposal or manuscript at a conference.

CHAPTER 32

What Does It Mean When an Agent Requests My Manuscript?

By Wendy Lawton

Strangely enough, requesting material based on an emailed query can mean something different than requesting material from a writer at a conference. The reason? A query sent "over the transom" is generally faceless. The agent considers the proposed project based on the merits of the query—unemotionally. That can be a good thing or a bad thing.

When an agent meets a writer at a conference, it can be much more complex. Let me offer you some context: When an agent agrees to attend a writers conference, the unspoken agreement is that he is open to considering new clients. Conferences depend on this possibility to offer perceived value. Writers often evaluate which conference to attend based on how many acquiring agents and editors will be there. Conference planners don't necessarily mean for this to happen, but this puts implicit pressure on agents and editors to request material. We are all so aware that writers need to justify the expense of a conference. That's not to say that when agents or editors request a manuscript, they aren't interested—they are or they wouldn't request it—but they may not be as realistic about the amount of work they are heaping on their plates as they would when at their desks reading faceless queries.

This is one of the reasons I sometimes attend a conference as an attendee, not as a faculty member. Then I have the luxury of interacting with writers sans any expectations. I can watch the writers I've had an eye on, and I can sit at a table and meet new ones. It often takes me many interactions over time to decide if I want to pursue a certain writer.

But, back to our main question . . . what does it mean when an agent meets with you at a conference and says, "Send the proposal" or even "Send the whole manuscript"? Each agent (and editor) is different. Personally, I've become more sensitive to avoid giving false hope so I'm stingy about offering to look over material. I have a very full practice, and while I always make room for someone exciting, I need to find ways at a conference to encourage good writers but still say no.

Do I regret this? You bet I do. I see writers all over the industry whose work I once turned down or writers to whom I never responded in time. I'm now part of their fan base. I read their fabulous published books, and I regret not being part of their team.

However, my first responsibility is to my current clients. It wouldn't be fair to brush them off while courting new writers. So when I request further material at a writers conference, I have every intention of evaluating that material and getting back to the writer in a timely fashion.

If, as a writer, I received a request for my proposal or the full manuscript at a writers conference, here's how I would decode that request:

- It's most likely a serious request based on liking the initial pitch and being interested in the writer. However, it is unknown whether the agent is being realistic about his ability to manage the additional work he is agreeing to evaluate.
- Or it could just be the general giddiness and I-can-do-it-all feeling that comes from letting an overworked agent out of the office. At a writers conference, we are predisposed to falling in love with ideas and writers. We're talking with colleagues and brainstorming possibilities. Heady stuff.
- It could also mean the agent has been meeting with writer after writer in fifteen-minute blocks all day long and has finally admitted he is exhausted and can no longer evaluate anything.

Therefore, he believes the best thing to do is to just see the work and evaluate later. The danger here is that he knows he is loading himself up with work, not taking into consideration the already critically backed-up workload at the office.

- It might mean the agent knows he can't evaluate fiction based on a query. He has to evaluate the writing of the entire novel. Novels can start out stunningly, but then sag in the middle or have an unsatisfying ending.
- Some agents and editors ask to see anything that may hold promise based on the pitch. (Sadly, some writers pitch like big leaguers while their writing isn't even ready for the farm team.)
- It might mean the agent is drawn to the writer himself and, regardless of the writing, wants to continue to explore. This is the power of meeting in person. These are the not-quite-ready writers that agents sometimes decide to sign, even earlier than normal, to mentor them. It's one of the values of a writing conference—the inexplicable connection that sometimes happens.

What then should a writer assume when an agent requests further material? The obvious—that he or she is interested in seeing more. And that's a very good thing. In a perfect world, if the agent were actively searching for a number of new clients, it would be a highly positive sign. In the real world, it means that you've risen above the vast majority of not-yet-published writers. You're attracting attention. There are still no guarantees, but it could be a very good sign.

And what should a writer do if he or she doesn't hear back? When the agent requests your material, ask when you might hear a response. Then, when the agent crosses that self-imposed deadline, it is appropriate to write a personable note nudging him or her. And repeat this every couple of months. Yes, I said *months*. I confess that I'm holding material more than a year old. It's the reality of my workload. And I've received some of the most gracious, charming nudges. Believe me, those writers make an impression.

How often is too often to nudge? "I don't want to bother the agent," you may say. Rethink this. Yes, you don't want to nudge too soon or too often—high maintenance is a huge turn-off—but your time and expectations are as valuable as the agent's. I don't know a single agent who brushes off writers as unimportant or expendable. It's just that we can't control fires that need to be extinguished or issues that require immediate attention. Contact the agent when it seems appropriate.

If that agent reacts badly, you've learned something very important. If that agent ignores your nudge, you know how overwhelmed he is, and you can decide to wait and nudge again or simply write him off.

Never, NEVER stop pitching your book to other agents or editors while waiting to hear from someone who requested your manuscript. We all understand you will continue marketing your work and we run the risk of losing out on representing you as we delay.

An important thing to remember: It is easy to get to the *no*. It takes only a couple of minutes for an agent to know something's not going to work. It takes a long time, however, to evaluate the *maybes*. Even though it is frustrating to wait and wait and wait, sometimes it can lead to the best outcome—even if that seems like a mixed signal.

CHAPTER 33

What Does It Mean When an Agent Informally Communicates with Me?

By Wendy Lawton

But what about informal contact with agents? Does it mean anything when an agent friends a writer on Facebook? How about when an agent seeks out a writer at a conference and knows that writer's name or something about what he's writing? How about if an agent is following you on Twitter? What about if he leaves comments on your blog?

Agents are human beings as well as professionals, and most of us love interacting with people both in person and in our online social networks. Those contacts may mean different things to different people, but here's a rule of thumb: Our business is highly relational. I won't represent someone I don't like. It doesn't matter how successful they are; if we don't connect, it won't work.

Part of being in the publishing community is getting to know writers and editors via social media. If an agent calls you by name at writers conferences or seems to seek you out, it's a very good thing. We meet a lot of people. When an agent remembers names and even what the writer is working on, it means you've made an impression. It probably signals an initial interest.

If an agent asks to friend you on Facebook, that's intentional. He or she is interested in you. If you are already agented, it may be because he or she has found your books and has become a fan. It may be that he or she doesn't know you're agented, or simply that he or she thinks you are interesting. Maybe you post the best recipes or great photos. Regardless, it's a relationship.

If you ask to friend agents on Facebook and they accept, it can mean something or it can mean nothing. They may just accept everyone whose name they recognize or who shows connections to the writing community. It doesn't matter. As they begin to follow you, your relationship can grow. And relationships are key, right?

What about Twitter? It's the same thing. It's just another place to connect. It can mean something or nothing. But it offers the possibility to get to know one another. Don't forget, as you retweet, the original tweeter gets a notification–a nice little shout-out. I have to admit that I am not as engaged on Twitter as I'd like to be, but I still notice the people who interact with me or retweet.

Do blog comments mean anything? If an agent goes to your blog, reads it, and comments, it certainly does mean something. None of the agents I know has time to idly surf the 'Net. If an agent has gone to your blog, that's intentional. He's interested in you for one reason or another. If he or she has commented, that's even more intentional since his or her name is linked with yours. Does it mean something more? There's no way to know, but it's a definite sign you're on the radar.

And speaking of blog comments, it never hurts for you to leave comments on the blogs of agents and editors who interest you. Blog comments are a way of entering into the conversation. To us it's a sign of engagement—a sign that the writer is not afraid of due diligence and is trying to learn as much as he or she can about us and the industry. You never know...we could reach out and ask for a proposal.

Which brings us to...

CHAPTER 34

Five Qualities Every Agent Looks for in a Potential Client

By Janet Kobobel Grant

Our agency receives thousands of queries every year, which means we have to say no to thousands of perfectly good writers as well as a fair portion of manuscripts that are, to be blunt, dreadful. But let's talk about the other side of the coin. Not the number of people we have to choose *not* to represent but those we select as our clients. What makes us decide to offer representation to a writer?

A Strong Sense of What Makes a Book Idea Compelling

Ever sit next to someone at church who is tone deaf but utterly enthusiastic about belting out the hymn or chorus? Writers can be tone deaf as well. By that I mean some writers have no sense of what readers will buy. So they come up with idea after idea that just isn't the right tune sung in the right way. As an agent, I'm looking for writers who can sing on key time after time. They have the ability to write about a topic in such a way that a reader wants to rush out to buy the book.

An Understanding of What Makes You Unique in the Marketplace

If you're writing romantic suspense, you are so not alone in that venture. What makes your work stand out from all the rest? As I read queries, I'm looking for what makes sense for this writer to be producing. If you have access to an investigator who specializes in gambling fraud, and you place your story at a casino run by an Indian tribe, you have a unique angle to write from.

Personality Match-Up

One of the aspects of agenting that I love is that I get to work with the people I want to work with. How cool is that? So when I consider representing someone, I want to be enthusiastic not only about the writing but also about the person. When I talk about a project to an editor, I don't discuss just the project; I sell the writer more than the project. So remember that if you present yourself in an overbearing way to an agent, that agent isn't going to fall to her knees and beg you to be her client. Nor is an agent likely to find a good candidate to represent in a writer who asks fifty questions for every answer. We've learned that such individuals will take up 80 percent of our time but not make 80 percent of our income. It just never turns out that way. Not that you shouldn't ask questions of a potential agent, but the person who worries an issue to death at the outset of the relationship generally is showing a lack of trust in the agent. And the author-agent relationship only works if you trust each other. I'm looking for writers I'm simpatico with.

Realistic Attitude about the Author's Role in Marketing and Publicity

I remember reading a quote from an editor in the 1950s that an author should be heard and not seen. In other words, you should hear the author through his writing, with the author as a sort of Wizard of Oz, working the great mechanism of his manuscript but never visible. Today, as you so well know, publishers want authors who are heard *and* seen. The author needs to be prepared to make a big marketing fuss when his or her title is released. I'm looking for clients who have applied themselves to building an e-mail list, a plan for promoting their books, and a significant online presence.

Stellar Writing

Remember the Pillsbury slogan, "Nothing says lovin' like somethin' from the oven"? Well, "Nothing says represent me like irresistible writing." Most agents are suckers for good writing. Sometimes I'll take on a person based on the writing—with the proviso that he or she will spend as long as necessary building that required platform before I pitch any projects to an editor. However, let the knowledge of our love of strong writing encourage you—beyond words.

Now Wendy's going to dip into greater detail of what we look for based on how experienced the writer is as well as some other factors.

CHAPTER 35

What Makes an Agent Say Yes?

By Wendy Lawton

A question asked of nearly every agent panel is, "What do you look for in a client?" We have heard this question answered by hundreds of people. Unfortunately, their answers often bear little resemblance to ours. What are some of those things we have heard? How about "a great book"? That's a given, but only part of the answer.

We've heard an incalculable number of writer-hopefuls bemoan that agents are only looking for published writers. Bzzzzzzz. Thanks for playing. Try again.

We've also read anti-agent bloggers who rant that agents are only trolling for A-list authors, as if we are only happy with a client list of solely *New York Times* best-sellers. Wrong again.

Our agency has identified four different levels of writers and what we look for at each level. First, we'll talk about the unpublished writer and a writer in the early stage of his/her career. Following that, we will address the well-published writer who's much in demand. And finally, we will talk about the challenges agents face in representing the writers with mega, A-list careers.

However, first let me clarify one other common misconception about agents we often hear at writers conferences: "Why is he here? He's not taking any new clients." I can't think of a single agent who is not open to a new client if the right person or right project came along, no matter how full his or her practice. There is always attrition. We have writers who retire. Others take a sabbatical to raise a family. Some clients leave us, and some we let go. An agent's list is always in flux for one reason or another.

Don't ever discount your dream agent because someone tells you her list is full. Every editor or agent dreams of being the one to discover the next Harper Lee, the next *To Kill A Mockingbird*. It takes no talent to sign a much-published author, but it takes a real eye to spot genius, and we are all addicted to that quest. Looking at my current client list, 48 percent of them came to me unpublished. Only 6.5 percent are still unpublished.

The Unpublished/Early-Stage Writer:

- **A near-perfect manuscript**. That goes without saying. The competition is steep so this is the prerequisite. That said, don't forget, taste is subjective. What one agent may reject, another may enthusiastically embrace. Unfortunately, we are seeing too many manuscripts too early. One editor uses the term *workmanlike* to describe them. It's all elbows. Every technique seems to jut out. The writing is self-conscious and overworked. The book that excites us is the product of a confident writer who has mastered the craft.
- **A distinctive voice**. We are looking for someone who will stand out in a crowded field. If you are writing nonfiction, we're looking for the writer who can become the go-to person for his category. In fiction, we look for the author who knows the difference between his own voice and each character's voice.
- **A professional attitude**. We're looking to build a team and want to work with writers who take their work seriously. Before becoming an agent, I spent more than two decades as an artist/designer in a tough industry. I never had patience for artistic sensibilities then. I'm not likely to change.
- **A winsome personality**. The dictionary defines *winsome* as "generally pleasing and engaging." Some agents love snarky

writers with attitude. Not me. Life is too short to have to clean up all the messes left in the wake of a clumsy personality. Since we get to choose whom we work with, we prefer the same kind of people we would choose as friends. People who add richness to our lives.

- **A hope and a future.** We look beyond the one book to a long-term career. We want to know what book number two and three and ten might be. We want a client with career potential. Does that mean we wouldn't consider a seventy-year-old writer? No. Some careers can be significant with one book.

Other qualities that may tip the scales include:

- **A great platform (for nonfiction).** Publishers are risk-averse these days. They are reluctant to publish nonfiction from unknown writers. Not saying it doesn't happen, but it is an uphill battle.
- **An impressive tribe.** A writer who can use social media with skill and finesse is very attractive these days.
- **A writer who will add to our community.** This one is specific to Books & Such. Unlike most agencies, we have built a collaborative community of clients. We gather for retreats, and we host online client forums to communicate and help each other. When we consider potential new clients, we take our agency's community into consideration. Is this someone who would fit in?

If you are a yet-unpublished writer looking for representation and a traditional publishing contract, take heart. You are pure potential. If you have a wonderful book, some agent is going to love discovering you and building your career from a clean slate.

Well-published Writer

- **A following and a built-in audience for each book.**
- **An ever-growing reader list.** This writer carefully cultivates those readers.
- **A distinctive brand.** He or she is well-known for it.

- **Recognized identity by most publishers.** And most of them would love to have a chance to make an offer for this writer's next book.
- **A regular rhythm to his or her writing, publishing on a set schedule.** We love representing the well-published client. From an agent's point of view, it's a great opportunity to take someone who's already doing everything right and strategize ways to move him or her up the best-selling rankings.

Perhaps the biggest obstacle in considering this writer is that most well-established writers are already agented. We agents have an unspoken agreement never to poach one another's clients so the only way we would be able to sign the well-published author is if he or she has left his agent for some reason, the agent has retired, or in rare cases, the author was never agented. We've had established writers who changed markets and looked for a specialist in that market. And we've had editors bring the client to us.

As for what we look for, it's the same as with other writers: great writing, voice, professionalism, and personality. It is always a special delight to sign a writer whose work you have long enjoyed as a reader.

Mega-Author

I represent a number of best-selling authors, one who regularly hits #1 on *The New York Times* best-sellers list. It is often said that all agents would love to have nothing but A-list authors. That's probably said by those who don't understand what is involved in representing an author with a big career. Representing best-selling authors is very different from representing most up-and-coming authors. The best-seller usually has a whole team, and every decision has a number of people invested in the outcome. Communication can be complicated. Weighing all the ramifications of every opportunity and each challenge is paramount. You'll often have far more opportunities than the author can ever entertain, but each possibility takes time to consider and either pursue or decline. When an agent has a handful of best-selling authors, just fielding possibilities and deflecting requests is time consuming.

So what do we look for when considering authors with big careers? The most important thing is deciding if we have time to do all of our clients justice. There is a finite number of authors we should take at each career level. The A-list author is no different. Before we seek to represent an author with a big career or even a nonprofit with an extensive publishing arm, we need to make sure we have the time, energy, and creativity to do it justice.

A newer author may wonder if it's wise to sign with an agent who represents the big names. Will he get less attention? That's a valid question, but one of the reasons I decided to write about the different career levels and what we look for in each is that a wise agent will build a practice that includes all levels. Our A-list clients give us leverage to negotiate better terms on our standard templates—benefiting all our clients since the publisher will use our agency's template for all of our clients, not just the A-list authors. Plus, we have certain leverage with publishers who would love to talk to us about our best-sellers. I rarely have a conversation about my in-demand clients in which I don't introduce the editor or publisher to one of my newer writers. Leverage. Ultimately it comes down to having a balanced list of clients, from beginner to best-seller.

The Inside Scoop on Your Proposal and Query

CHAPTER 36

Creating a Compelling Proposal

By Wendy Lawton

Writers have plenty of questions about proposals, but first things first.

What Is a Proposal?

- Your book proposal is actually your business plan. Like a traditional business plan, it will outline the product (i.e., the book itself); the customer (i.e., the reader); the author, including his or her past sales history; the marketing plan; the competition; and a sample of the product.
- The book proposal is the blueprint of choice in publishing. Many an author wishes he could just submit his book and let the work speak for itself. However, publishing is a business. When an author submits his book to an agent or a publisher, he's asking for a business partner—someone to help him manufacture, market, and distribute the product. It's going to require a significant investment of money on the part of the publisher. The proposal answers, in advance, all the questions the decision makers will ask.
- Much of the content of the proposal is the raw material the publisher will eventually use in marketing the book. The

author bio, the book description, the hook, and the back cover copy all come from the proposal.

- The proposal ensures that your brilliant idea is communicated through layer after layer of decision makers. Let's say you want to skip the trouble of a formal proposal and you communicate your vision verbally to an agent. That agent then communicates to an acquisitions editor. The editor must sell the editorial team and then the publishing committee. If the book is acquired, the information needs to be communicated to the marketing department and then to the sales team. The salespeople then have to sell the book to the buyers, who in turn promote the book to bookstore personnel. Finally, the book is sold to the reader. That's nine layers. If just a little excitement or detail leaks at every layer, you'll hit ho-hum long before the sales team. A powerful proposal carries that excitement through every layer of the publishing house and provides the detailed information the marketing department needs to take it the rest of the way.

For Whom Do You Write a Proposal?

- For agents and editors. This goes without saying. This is how we make decisions.
- For the author. This may surprise you, but the proposal is invaluable to you. Many a book has been reshaped or abandoned during the process of detailing the competition. As you do the hard work of building the business plan for the book, it helps to creatively shape it, whether it is fiction or nonfiction. The work you do on this end of the project will save you much aimless wandering on the other end.

What Does a Good Proposal Do?

- It answers all the questions a publishing committee might ask.
- It gives a solid overview of the book.
- It tells why the book is needed.

- It tells why the book is unique.
- It tells why the author is the person to write the book.

Is There a Standardized Proposal Format?

There is no shortage of material on how to format a proposal. At our agency we've developed a Style Guide for our clients' proposals. We like to think that when an editor gets a proposal in our signature format, it makes them smile, thinking of all the great books they've bought from us in the past that have looked similar. But if you are creating a proposal on your own, just make sure it has all the important parts and looks professional.

Can You Be Creative?

It's always a risk. We agents have all seen too many fancy proposals that have no substance. However, if your book calls for some creativity, and you are willing to take the risk…

What If You're Beyond Having to Do a Proposal in Your Career?

The proposal is a tool, as much for you as for the agent and the editor. It's like a builder saying, "I've built so many houses, I don't need a plan or blueprints on this one. The subs all know what I do more or less." Scary.

Now, let's take a look at the details in a compelling proposal.

CHAPTER 37

Book Proposals in a Nutshell

By Wendy Lawton

Confession: All my life I've been a rule-follower. I obey all posted signs. I follow the letter of the law. I feel most comfortable with clear, unambiguous rules. I'm neither a maverick nor a risk-taker.

When I was a new writer, I studied book after book and article after article about book proposals. I took at least a dozen different workshops on proposal writing—fiction, nonfiction, children's. And you know what? The more I learned, the more confused I became. When agents say "table of contents" in a proposal, do they refer to the table of contents of the book or of the proposal? (Hint: You'll see both.)

Long before I became an agent, I cried "uncle" when it came to the rules of a good book proposal. For every carved-in-stone rule you find, you will also find an agent or an editor who'll contradict that rule. So what's a writer to do?

Here are my common sense generic rules for creating a book proposal:

- If you are preparing a proposal for your agent, use the agency style sheet. If you are unagented and doing the proposal for a specific house, see if it has a sample proposal on its website to use as a guideline.

- Strip away all the voodoo that surrounds the proposal mystique. You are simply writing a business plan for the book. You'll want to present the book in the best light and answer any potential questions about the book or about you, the author, in advance.
- Don't be annoying or cute. Be professional.
- Be distinctive (this doesn't mean fancy fonts or decoration).
- Summarize the book succinctly. I personally like to see both a two- or three-sentence hook and a back-cover-copy-sized summary.
- Understand that the proposal for a novel and a nonfiction book will be different. The novel will need a synopsis while the nonfiction book gets an annotated table of contents, chapter-by-chapter.

Elements of a Generic Fiction Proposal

- **Title:** Yes, it's true that the working title may not stick, but you still need to come up with a superb title. See Janet's thoughts on titles in Chapter 16. After all, even though you may not get to use the title to hook your eventual reader, it does have to catch the eye and imagination of professionals.
- **Promo pitch (or hook):** This describes the book in one or two compelling sentences. While this may be the hardest thing you ever write, it is important for both fiction and nonfiction. You'll often see these hooks near the top of the back cover, or sometimes even on the front cover. Look at a few books on your shelves and see if you can pick out the hooks. Does it make you want to read the book? This will be the luscious appetizer—the tiniest bite of all.
- **Back cover-like copy:** This is the next biggest bite and is an easy one to figure out. Just get a stack of books and study what back cover copy looks like. What does it accomplish? Remember, each little piece, each component, may be used for different promotional purposes. Take time with these. You'll

see the words you select over and over again. This might be the teaser that goes to the sales team along with the manuscript. It might be used to develop ad copy. A version of it might even end up as your book's back cover.

- **Genre:** Make sure you figure out the best genre description of your book, but refrain from incorporating too many combinations or fusions. Remember that this information is so the store will know where to shelve your book. Study the stacks in the bookstore if you are unsure. Turn books over and you will see how they are categorized. If you'd like to dig more deeply into this, check out the BISAC (Book Industry Subject and Category) codes online.
- **Audience:** You need to know who is most likely to read your book and communicate this in your proposal (and don't say "everybody"). This is a list of the core readers for your book, not the people on the fringes.
- **Manuscript info:** Here's where you give the details—word count, when it will be done, the publication rights offered, and what else is included in the proposal.
- **Synopsis**: Hit the high points. Don't get bogged down in details. Don't be afraid to let your voice creep in. You want to give a flavor of the book but don't try to make this a literary work of art. Someone once told me that if you want to study the art of the synopsis, buy a *Soap Opera Digest* magazine off the rack at your grocery store and see how it boils down a week's worth of soap opera action into a few short paragraphs. Be sure to include the ending. Your editor wants to see how you work everything out. A good synopsis is the blueprint of your novel. It will help the editor gauge the storyline and decide whether it will make a compelling read. Plus it gives you a map of where the story is going. As for how long to make it, you'll have to research your target proposal recipient. Some publishers want a two-page synopsis; others want a very detailed synopsis. Read details on synopses online to get a

sense of what to include and the tone of a good synopsis. The synopsis is your biggest bite next to the sample chapters or a full manuscript.

- **Market Comparison**
  - **Give a point of reference:** This is another way to help the agent or editor get a handle on your book. **However, do not name blockbusters.** "My book is like a combination of *Heaven Is for Real* because it features a father and a son, *Girl with a Dragon Tattoo* because it includes a disquieting basement scene, and Harry Potter because characters travel via British trains." (Can't you just picture the editorial team rolling their eyes?) Remember, your job is to capture the essence of your book and compare and contrast it to something that (1) should appeal to a similar demographic, (2) shares some thematic similarities, and (3) will give the agent or editor some context for forecasting sales possibilities. When you pick a phenomenon like Harry Potter, it's silly to offer it as a comparison. The appeal and trajectory of that series is akin to a hundred-year flood. It's not going to come around again in our lifetimes. These kinds of wild comparisons not only are useless, but also indicate faulty reasoning and magical thinking. Not professional. Not helpful. **Also, refrain from saying, "There's nothing like this on the market."** To some extent that's true of every book. Yes, you are unique, so no one has ever captured what you will capture in your book, but saying that defeats the purpose of what we are trying to do with a competitive analysis. Besides, if it were true, you'd be hard-pressed to convince anyone that there would be a place for your book on the shelf or even a market for it.
  - **Show that you know what is already out there:** If, say, you are writing a young adult dystopian novel and you fail to address how your book differs from *Hunger Games*, an

editor would wonder how much you know about YA and how well you know your readers.

- **Help the editor or agent get a feel for how well your book may sell:** As you list the books that are similar, you'll give ISBN numbers for each (which are found on the copyright page of every book). If your book goes to committee, sales figures will be compiled by the acquiring editor for each one of those books to give a point of reference for the scope of the potential market.

- **Author biographical information.**
  - **A great bio**: Make it interesting. If your writing is quirky, let the bio reflect that. If you write history, give a nod to that in your bio. In other words, make sure your bio is a representative reflection of your book and your writing. Include any contest wins and awards. Go easy on the personal stuff.
  - **Photo**: The jury is out on this. I've heard some editors mock this practice, but I've had several editors or publishers tell me how much they liked putting a face with the name. I am ever aware that there is ageism at play here, so if I had an 88-yer-old debut novelist, I may not offer the photo lest the publisher think the author won't be around long enough to build a significant career.
  - **Past (or selected) publication history**: This is very important. You'll want to end this section with a graph giving actual numbers sold. No, you can't fudge. If you have no publication history, omit this part. Don't try some fancy footwork. Also, don't include any academic writing. If you've published both adult and children's books, include only the numbers that are relevant to your current project.
- **Blurb possibilities:** If writers have offered to blurb (endorse) your novel, have a paragraph that lists those writers along with the title and publisher of their latest (or greatest) novel.

Remember, the best endorsers are those with whom you may share an audience. If you are yet unpublished, don't ask published authors to write blurbs for you now. They are overwhelmed with requests. Once you are contracted, it's soon enough to ask. Just ask them now if they'll consider endorsing your manuscript after you have a contract, and list the names of those who are open to possibly endorsing.

- **Author marketing ideas:** Be sure to outline the scope and size of your social network. Most editors now see that as the primary sphere of influence for an author. Some publishers don't believe novelists need to include this segment in their proposals since it's so hard for debut writers to build ways to connect with potential readers. Other publishers insist on it.
- **Three sample chapters**: This is where the writer gets to show off his or her writing skills. All I can say is relax. If you are proposing a novel, just tell the story in your own unique voice.

Elements of a Nonfiction Proposal

- **A great bio**: Emphasize why you are the perfect person to write this book. Study other excellent bios in published books if in doubt. Make sure to give your credentials if the book you are writing requires your track record.
- **Photo:** See above.
- **Past publication history**: See above. Published articles on your subject are important as well.
- **Influencers and endorsers:** If you have the imprimatur of leaders in your field, that could well be a tipping point. Be careful not to overwhelm, but a good solid list of recognizable names can be gold.
- **Author marketing ideas:** Here's where you have to pull out all the stops. If you are a speaker, detail that, giving your upcoming schedule. Publishers like to quantify this. For example: "I speak to groups, both inspirational and motivational, about

25 times a year, including two platform appearances and one stadium event. Altogether, I speak to more than 100,000 people annually." Talk about the size and scope of your social network. List some of those who will be willing to influence potential readers on your behalf. If you've been on national television and radio, outline those in detail.

- **Competitive analysis:** As with fiction, you need to identify the titles the potential reader would purchase rather than yours. Or books that help the agent or editor understand what makes your manuscript unique from others on the subject. Be sure to list the major works in the subject of your book. If you were writing a nonfiction book about relationships and communication and did not reference *The Five Love Languages* (a long-time best-seller on the topic), that would show a huge hole in your knowledge of what's key in your supposed field.
- **Chapter-by-chapter summary**: When writing a nonfiction book, it is paramount to let the agent or editor see how you plan to develop the text. You do this by creating a chapter-by-chapter summary. You list each chapter by title (or number if you are not titling the chapters). Next to each chapter you tell what that chapter will cover. An editor should be able to see how you are developing the book and building the content.
- **Three sample chapters:**
    - Most editors and agents confess that when they open a proposal, they skip over it at first and turn right to the sample chapters. As one editor put it, "If the author can't write, why waste my time on the business aspects of the book?"
    - Our agency requests three sample chapters with a proposal, but Your Mileage May Vary—meaning it may be different for individual agents and editors.
    - With nonfiction, it need not be the first three chapters. However, if you cherry-pick, it may raise questions. Was

the first chapter weak? Does this mean the book doesn't really get good until the sixth chapter? And, since the first chapters set up what you intend to accomplish through the rest of the book, they generally will be the way to put your best foot forward.

- We like the whole proposal to weigh in at about fifty pages. Once again, this can vary between agencies and editors.
- The proposal and sample chapters should be in one single file. (Don't get me started about multiple files for proposals and manuscripts!) No fancy formatting. You are offering a sampling of the text, not of an interior book design. If you have a sidebar or another feature, simply label it such and include it in manuscript form.
- Don't make the mistake of over-editing the first three chapters. We often see manuscripts in which the first three chapters have the very life edited out of them. The voice and ease of writing doesn't show until chapter four. Or, some authors pay to have the first three chapters edited, and they end up not even being representative of the author's writing. I also see writing that has been what I call "workshopped to death." That's where the critique group has worked over every word so many times that the writing wears you out while reading it. Each simple word is pumped up to the level of purple prose. All I can say is relax. Write clearly and simply.
- Typos and grammar mistakes should never be allowed to slip through. At this stage, they are a red flag and distracting.

As for all the formatting rules, do the best you can to craft a clear, clean proposal. Most experts will tell you that the business part of the proposal is single-spaced, while the sample chapters are double-spaced in regular manuscript format. (You can't go wrong with 12 point Times New Roman.)

Remember, your goal is to give a clear picture of the book, the reason the reader will want to purchase the book, who the author is, and what the author can do to partner with the publisher to make the book a success. And while it may be annoying to follow such a strict format, it will help you to develop the book and keep your voice focused.

CHAPTER 38

Read the Market

By Wendy Lawton

Do you feel lost when experts tell you that you need to be a book-marketing guru? We often hear from writers that knowing the potential competition for their books is the hardest thing about doing a proposal. But reading the market is an important part of writing books that will sell. Here's why:

- You need to know where your proposed book will sit on the shelf in a store so that you can fill a need, plug a hole, or offer a different voice from everyone else out there.
- You need to know who else is writing similar novels. Novelists need to be able to supply readers with comparables. "If you like the books of Jane Doe, you'll probably like mine." (And don't worry that someone else has written something similar. Think of your own reading patterns. When you finish a great medieval historical, you don't want to leave that world. You look around for another great medieval, right?)
- You need to know who else has recently addressed your nonfiction subject and how they approached it. If a *New York Times* best-selling author just wrote on your subject, you might want to wait awhile before proposing this book. Remember, when someone walks in the bookstore and asks for a book on XYZ, the front-liners—bookstore salespeople—are going to immediately think of the A-list book on that subject.

- Or you need to know if there's been a recent glut of books on this subject. Publishers will hold off if the category is full.

So . . . agreed, right? Reading the market is essential for authors. But how does one do it? Let me offer a few suggestions:

- **Read shelves**. Spend time in the stores. Pay attention to which books are cover out. How many copies does the store have? All of these tell a tale and help you to read the market.
- **Talk to librarians.** Nobody knows books as librarians do. Granted, they may not be as current as the market is, but they know what's out there, and they know which books get checked out most.
- **Talk to bookstore front-liners**. Front-liners are the ones who direct readers to books. Find out what they know.
- **Study Goodreads** and other online reading apps. There's much information on the market tucked into these online communities.
- **Read magazines** like *Romantic Times*. These periodicals are not trade magazines. They go to readers. The reviewers are avid readers.
- **Spend time on Amazon, B & N, or publishers' websites**. These resources are pure gold for writers. Not only can they help you in reading the market and knowing what's out there, but they can help you with the "readers who purchased this, have also purchased . . ." comparisons.
- **Collect anecdotal evidence.** This is the fun way. Always ask, "Read any good books lately?" "How did you hear about it?" "Where do you buy your books?" Everyone you meet is a potential resource, and everyone loves to talk about what he or she is reading.
- **Identify typical readers** and separate them from professional readers. This is essential. When we hang with other professionals—publishers, editors, writers—we are not talking to run-of-the-mill readers. We need to always keep that in mind.

That's just the tip of the iceberg. But it's a great place to start.

CHAPTER 39

Focusing the Proposal: How an Author and an Agent Work as a Team

By Janet Kobobel Grant

One of my clients sent me a proposal for a complex project with lots of elements to explain in the proposal, including the possibility of a video accompanying the book. She had a powerful idea of how to make the story vivid for the reader. But she had to visit the locale of the book and conduct several more interviews before she could envision its precise structure. Therefore, the proposal was a challenge to create.

When I first read the proposal, I realized that the order in which the elements of the project were presented muddled the book's structure rather than clarifying it. So I did major cutting and pasting rather than try to communicate to my client what needed to be done. It was simpler just to do the work. I also added quite a bit to the proposal to help to explain the book's idea.

I've found that often an author doesn't know how to talk about his or her project in the most compelling way. I see it as my job to massage the proposal to highlight what I think are the strong selling points. I always expect the author to do his or her best to figure out the book's hook and its uniqueness, but when the author fails, I step in.

I invested days in honing this proposal, but I asked my client to rework the sample chapters. They had the essence of what they needed to be, but I thought they were overly literary to the point of obfuscation and wordiness. I did some editing but mostly provided direction to the author.

A short time later, the proposal was back to me along with thanks for the work I'd done. I read over the chapters and found them gaining ground, but they hadn't arrived at their destination yet. So I dug out my editing pen (figuratively, of course) and went to work. I *really* overhauled the chapters. By the time I finished, they gleamed.

I sent the proposal off to my client so she could see what I had done. Then I worried. Would she be upset that I had used such a heavy editing hand? Would she think I had exceeded my role?

I'm thankful to say that she responded with a clever e-mail about her overwrought writing, recognizing I had pulled the chapters into the shape she would have formed, if she knew how to get them there.

What can you learn from this back and forth between the author and the agent?

- The author was able to see us as a team, putting together the most effective proposal possible.
- She was responsive to suggestions for change rather than defensive.
- She recognized that I was helping to take the project to where she wanted it to go.

When an author and an agent work together hand in hand, it's a beautiful thing. And everyone benefits.

I do need to add that I want my clients to have the freedom to say, "Um, that's not what I intended." I'm not a mind reader, and I can misstep or overstep.

Agents love it when they can read a proposal and proclaim, "Perfection!" But if the proposal's not there yet, I'm willing to help make it so. That's a quality to look for in an agent. Some agents will glance at your proposal and sample chapters and then send them off to editors without taking the time to critically examine how the project is presented. You do, after all, only have one chance to get a yes from an editor.

CHAPTER 40

Writing a Winsome Query

By Janet Kobobel Grant

Once you've assembled your idea, given it a strong title, and done your homework on making a proposal that pops, it's time to write your query.

The word *query* means "question." You're asking the agent the question, "Do you want to see my proposal and sample chapters (or full manuscript, if you've written a novel)?"

Even though the query is the first communication you'll have with an agent, note the order in which these elements have been pulled together. Rather than jumping into writing a query, you've taken your time to force yourself to define the project. You know so much about it because you've made sure you have a unique idea, an enticing title, and a strong sense of the book's structure and audience, and you've given thought to how you'll promote it. *Now* you're ready to write a winsome query.

Your first sentence in the query is important because, just as your book's first sentence, it sets the tone, highlights a strong point, and launches all that follows with a great ta-da! The challenge is not overdoing that sentence, yet not being bland.

I don't respond well to queries that open with promises of my becoming rich by representing the project or to queries that suggest the book is the most stupendous story since Dickens. Never oversell!

But do:

- **Start out with your strongest point.** If you're an authority on a topic, tell me so right up front. If you've self-published the book and sold 15,000 copies in six months, I'll want to hear about that. If your novel has a unique twist, tell me. For example, "*Intertwined* is a modern re-telling of Shakespeare's Romeo and Juliet." Do you see how quickly I can decide if that idea interests me?
- **Show you are capable of writing a cogent argument for the reasons your book should be successful.** Be realistic here; be careful to present a well-reasoned thought rather than being bombastic. Statistics can be helpful. The number of women on prescription drugs for depression, for example, would give the agent an idea of how significant your book on dealing with depression could be.
- **Present yourself as intelligent and authentic.** Avoid all appearances of being a snake-oil salesman. Agents want to work with people they genuinely like. Sometimes we can tell by the query that this is a person we would enjoy meeting. Obviously, we'll want to make a more substantial connection with a writer to confirm that sense, but this is what you're striving for in your query.
- **Don't apologize.** Don't start out with, "I've never been published," or "My agent just dropped me," or "I've submitted my project to every publisher I can imagine, and they've all turned me down." Now, if an agent involves you in conversation about your project, you do need to be forthcoming about these issues, but you don't need to address them in your query. These confessions come later.
- **Tell what the book's hook is, who the audience is, how you can reach that audience, and a brief paragraph about who you are and why you're qualified to write the book.**
- **Be sure to tell what genre or category your book fits in.** This shows you understand what you're writing and for whom.

- **Tell me the word coun**t. It informs me as to whether you understand how long a book in your genre or category should be.
- **Don't forget to mention the title.** If that seems obvious, just guess why I've put it on the list…

Now Wendy will provide you with more of the nuts and bolts about a winsome query.

CHAPTER 41

Do You Need to Know Each Agent's Query Guidelines?

By Wendy Lawton

Agent websites are filled with instructions on how and how not to query. Nearly every writers conference offers a session or two on queries and pitching.

If someone had unlimited time and decided to collect all the tips and all the rules from every tweet, blog and website, I'm guessing those tips could fill a book. Or two. And interestingly enough, I'll bet every rule would be contradicted a number of times.

So what's a writer to do?

Here are my own common sense generic rules for queries:

- If you want to increase your chances of getting that all-important proposal request from your target agent, **read the guidelines on his or her website and follow them**. If, on the other hand, you are sending to scores of agents and don't want to take the time to individualize the queries and the protocol to meet the agency guidelines, just realize that you may be hurting your chances on a percentage of these. It may be worth the trade-off to you.

- If you decide to use a **query service**, just be aware that all those queries are formatted the same, and they strip you of any distinctiveness. We can spot them at first glance. Again, it can lower your odds.
- **Let your query style match the voice of your book.** If you write humor, let the query show a lighthearted touch here and there. If it is academic, the query needs to reflect that.
- **Try not to be annoying.** For instance, opening with a rhetorical question has become cringe-worthy to those of us who read queries.
- The things that are important, aside from telling us what the story or book is about, are **whether you've been referred and if you've published successfully previously** (especially if you have a strong readership or fabulous sales numbers).

Do the best you can to craft a query that makes it difficult for the agent to say "no thanks." And let your e-query be only one of many methods you're pursuing to obtain an agent or a publishing contract. You also need to:

- Meet editors and agents in person at writers conferences
- Submit directly to those publishers still open to un-agented queries
- Enter contests judged by agents and editors
- Continue to connect with published writers who may make introductions

Would I disqualify an otherwise excellent query because it did not follow our guidelines? Of course not. Agents are in the business of trying to find bright new talent. The guidelines are just our way of obtaining the info we need to ferret out the exciting stuff in the most efficient way.

CHAPTER 42

#QueryFail: Clever Queries

By Wendy Lawton

When you're sending a query, don't try to be clever. It can fall flat. The only exception to this rule is if you are writing humor. Then your query needs to reflect that. Other than that, beware. Let me show you some carefully redacted clever queries.

> *My name is [John Doe], and I'm an enigma. I've also written a [umpteen] word manuscript or else this query would really be a waste of your, mine, and our time. I believe in capitalism but don't want to work for the man. I believe in freedom but don't want to fight for it. I'm against war but stay silent, mostly, on America's practices of exploitation. I grew up in an anti-Communist America, but think the government should help me out while staying out of my personal life. In short, I am conflicted.*
>
> *<SNIP a ton of superfluous details>*
>
> *Suffice it to say, my [describes book]. It is stupid in its brilliance and brilliant in its stupidity. . .tragic in its verisimilitude and verisimilitudey in its tragicness. . . . It is both an indictment of the vapidity of pop culture and a sentimental journey through a mind obsessed with it. In short, my new friend, my book saves lives.*

<SNIP another two pages of stuff>

Right now—at this very moment—I am entering the stretch run of my college career. I am [00] years old and am about to graduate from the [university]. (The aforementioned dog is graduating from the [another university], with a degree in aeronautics or barking or something it's probably barking, which is where we dropped her off)

Okay. Clever? Did it appeal to you? Do you see the risk the writer took in trying to be edgy? Picture an agent trying to squeeze in queries at the end of a long day. This doesn't work. Clever is a huge risk.

So how about this clever one. It's a reply to the email I sent a writer telling him he just queried the wrong address and offering him the correct address:

Whatever. You have a "finger" right? You can send it cant you? Geeeese. Just forward the message. This is one of the greatest stories EVER told. I don't have time to waste.

Now that's certainly a humorous way to endear yourself to an agent. Or how about this one?

It's almost not fair. Actually it isn't fair. It's so not fair. Here I am, left with a page, one page, just one page, to grab your attention and set aside my query letter from the rest of the hundreds and maybe thousands that you get on a weekly basis, so you contact me back to read my manuscript. But that's what they say about life right? It's not fair, or is it that it's like a box of chocolates? No, that was Forest Gump, good movie huh? If it was a true story then it'd be a great movie. I wanna be like Forest Gump, but I'm not slow, so I'll be the smart Forest Gump and go on and do great things (have I gotten your attention yet?) Well If not then let me keep going....

You don't know me, as an author, but you should. You know why you should? Well do ya? I'll tell ya why, because I am a best-selling author. That's right a best-selling author, if this was 8 to 12 months from now. Ooops, I know I'm not supposed to say that, boast about the books. So I just broke the rules of querying an agent with that one. But hey I gotta get your attention some how right?

Well now let me stop making you laugh. . .be boring and briefly tell you about those several books I have.

Does this help you to understand why agents get cranky about queries? I'm not disparaging these writers. I understand they are trying to find a way to be distinctive, but humor is subjective and therefore risky when querying.

Don't do it.

CHAPTER 43

#QueryFail: TMI

By Wendy Lawton

I believe it's important for me to know something about the author via the query. When I agree to represent a new client, I am representing that writer for a whole career, not just one book. I need to know who you are and what you've done. That said, however, it is important not to give TMI (too much information). Keep it succinct. Again, pique my interest.

What is TMI? Let me give you a few real-life examples–carefully redacted so as not to identify the writer.

> *Besides the book I have published (not a good publisher I ended up getting, I was young in the industry without much knowledge or business experience) . . .*

Don't denigrate another agent or publisher in your query letter. There's enough time later to do a post-mortem of a failed book or a troubled agent relationship, but when you are just meeting someone it comes off as judgmental, blaming, and whiny. Your assessment may very well be true, but you need a deeper relationship to risk the way it sounds.

> *As you can see from the following material, my wife and I are desperate. Our bankruptcy is in Federal Appeals Court (headed for the Supreme Court?), and our attorney, [name of attorney]*

is aware of my intellectual property [name of manuscript] has advised me to offer it on the open market. Perhaps you can help.

Mentioning your financial need could well be the death knell for a query, no matter how wonderful the book. This industry moves slowly, and a potential agent knows that; like any new business, writing books will probably take a number of years for an author to financially break even. A client who is financially strapped tends to write too fast out of desperation and make terrible decisions out of need that ultimately harm a long-term career plan.

My name is [Jane Doe], I am a 41-year-old divorced mom, (former victim of emotional and verbal abuse) dental hygienist, lecturer, home sex toy party sales person and author. My X husband lost his job 1 week after our "D" was final. After years of hearing you're nothing, how wrong he was.

Even ignoring the sex toy sales job (way, way TMI), an agent would see this query as unprofessional. It's sad, but too much drama tends to get in the way of a writing career. Yes, we all have stuff in our past, but your query doesn't need to share everything. However, if you are writing a book in which your personal experiences form the basis of your expertise, that's a different issue. Just be sure to be professional and emotionally detached in a query.

I am a new writer and have never, ever submitted any work to any agent or publisher. But a worthwhile idea just popped into my head one day. I have been working on that idea for 2 months now and am planning on completing it by the fall. It is an excellent idea.

As for marketing the story, I was hoping that would be your expertise; otherwise, if I had enough money, I would publish it myself. I would make it a paperback, so it would be more affordable to parents with young children. It would have glossy pages, so their sticky fingers wouldn't ruin the book. The book should be at least an 8-1/2 by 11 or larger, so it is visually appealing to the boys and girls, and with large type so they can read along to some extent. To add interactive play with the book, you could sell it with a stuffed toy that is accompanied with outfits.

Most agents do not want this type of specific marketing, book design detail in a query. Save it for the proposal. Though most agents do help some with marketing ideas, that is *not* our expertise. Also, by saying that if she had money she would self-publish, it makes it appear that traditional publishing is this author's last choice. And, above all, do not give directions for designing the book. That would even be presumptuous of an agent to say to a publisher.

I read only one book, when I was 6 years old, and it was 12 pages long. I went to the kindergarten, and read them my first and last book. Sure, I had to read when I went to school, and at work, but I would skim through everything and look for the most important things in the book, or in any manual. I have paid the consequences in my life, by not reading anyone's books in my life. I am telling you the truth; I haven't even read an entire magazine before!

This one was too sad. Someone who doesn't read is pretty much disqualified to write a book. It is imperative to read widely in your category or your genre. If you are not a reader, you cannot be a writer.

In a way, you could say these authors went over the top with their bios. But writers can go over the top in their queries any number of other ways.

CHAPTER 44

#QueryFail: Over the Top

By Wendy Lawton

The last two chapters have focused on avoiding the too-clever query and the too-much-information query. Now we're going to wind up #QueryFail by looking at queries that fail because they are filled with hyperbole and cringe-worthy braggadocio.

Here are some quotes from actual queries I've received:

Over the past nine years, I've been working on a project to bring world peace.

Hmm. World peace. It would be wonderful if it were to happen, but too often those things are out of our control as authors. My advice to this writer would be not to over-promise.

We're talking about a literary masterpiece spanning over 1,000 pages.

Try to avoid using words like *masterpiece* when describing your own work. I won't even go into the impossibility of the book length.

I can assure you, if you pass this opportunity by, you will grieve the loss of millions of dollars. I must stress, however, that I must absolutely find the best book deal possible, and I will be contacting several literary agencies in order to find it.

I don't think I even need comment on this one. Don't dangle the commission you expect the agent to make from your work–it comes off as crass. The agent is the one who knows the business and has a good sense of the relative value of projects.

What must I do for you to take on my book and run with my idea (When you get the full scope of my idea, you will be amazed, I promise you!)?

Rather than be "amazed" in the future, it would have been nice to have been given the scope of the book in the query letter. Too many query letters talk about the book in superlatives but neglect to ever say what it is about!

I think Ralph Waldo Emerson summed it up best: "The mark of the man of the world is absence of pretension. He does not make a speech; he takes a low business-tone, avoids all brag, is nobody, dresses plainly, promises not at all, performs much, speaks in monosyllables, hugs his fact. He calls his employment by its lowest name and so takes from evil tongues their sharpest weapon. His conversation clings to the weather and news, yet he allows himself to be surprised into thought and the unlocking of his learning and philosophy." Such a low-key approach is welcomed in queries, especially in light of the over-the-top ones we receive way too often.

PART FIVE

The Inside Scoop on How the Author and the Agent Work Together

CHAPTER 45

What Does an Agent Do?

By Janet Kobobel Grant

Some jobs look pretty much the same one day as they do the next. That's seldom true for a literary agent. One day can be all about phone calls. Another day I might not speak on the phone once. One day might be focused on negotiating a contract or readying a proposal. Another could consist of a single emergency that derails the day as I look for a fix.

I've arbitrarily picked a day from last week to give you a glimpse into a typical day in the life of an agent, which provides a sense of what an agent does.

7:00 a.m.: Rise and bleary-eyed feed the dog, eat breakfast, dress and take a quick walk. (Confession: Not every day starts with exercise. That depends on how early I start phone calls, the weather, and, well, my inclination.)

9:00 a.m.: At my desk and implementing my new discipline of spending no more than 30 minutes on **social media**. I check to make sure our blog has posted, read the blog and comments; zip over to Facebook and catch up on the latest news on my feed, adding a post of my own; move on to Twitter, where I read any direct messages, glimpse at my Twitter feed and do a bit of tweeting and retweeting. My social media engagement is to stay tuned to clients, other authors I'm interested in, and what's happening in the industry.

9:30 a.m.: Read **priority e-mails** from clients, editors and other agents.

Mark those that will require considerable time (attached proposal, contract to negotiate, or complex situation with a client). Respond to all priority emails that can be answered fairly quickly. (Since more than a hundred emails that require responses await me each morning, even a quick pass through them can take several hours.)

11:00 a.m.: **Call a client** for a catch-up conversation. We haven't talked in several months and have on our agenda:

- Update each other on developments on a film option for a series.
- Strategize upcoming meetings with film producers for a movie that will go into production later in the year.
- Look over list of possible book projects for the client to develop. Prioritize the list and brainstorm strong hooks for each.

12:00 p.m.: Work on **e-mails** that had required careful consideration before responding.

12:50 p.m.: Wendy, who is at a conference, calls to ask me the title of a book she wants to talk about during her workshop but can't recall the exact wording.

1:00 p.m.: **Reschedule weekly meeting** with another agent in our agency because she is at the computer store, trying to get her laptop to function correctly. Take the unexpected break in my day to work on a **publisher's contract**. I've already spent an hour on it the day before and had marked clauses that I wanted to suggest changes on. Work hard on alternate wording and what I want to delete, along with providing the contracts administrator with my rationale for the changes. Don't make it through the process before my next scheduled call. . .

2:00 p.m.: An executive editor calls me to explain a **legal complication** he's encountered regarding a project he made an offer on a week ago. He tells me his idea for a solution, and I respond with why I think the solution has its own problems. We agree that he'll return to his legal department to express my concerns.

2:15 p.m.: I take a quick break to make a pot of tea, which is an afternoon office tradition. Often the mail has arrived at this point. I **look over any payments** for our clients to be sure they're correct and to mark the monies on our payment tracking sheet. If royalty statements had been in the mail, I would set those aside for when I had time to concentrate to study them over and to make sure all titles had been reported and that the statements were accurate. Because we receive statements for multiple clients from each publisher, this is an excellent opportunity to see trends regarding what this publisher is doing well and which of our clients are seeing significant growth in sales and which are seeing significant decline in sales. Action needs to be taken for either situation for a client.

2:30 p.m.: I look over the proposal and sample chapters for a **potential new client** for one of our agency's agents. I see several pluses but also have some concerns about whether the writer is ready for representation. I create an email and send it to the agent for us to discuss later.

3:00 p.m.: Time for my **weekly meeting** with Books & Such agent Rachelle Gardner. We discuss some of the challenges we've each been facing (including my concerns about the contract I'm working on) and brainstorm ways to deal with them. Being part of a team is an important aspect of how our agency functions; none of us has to face complex situations alone.

4:00 p.m.: Read a **client's fiction synopsis** to determine if the idea is strong enough for the client to move on to sample chapters. Thumbs up on this one!

5:00 p.m.: **Back to e-mails**, checking on new ones and reading lower priority ones from earlier in the day.

6:00 p.m.: Take a dinner break.

7:00 p.m.: **Back to work on the contract**, finishing my suggested changes and e-mailing it to the publisher's contracts administrator.

8:00 p.m.: Quit work and watch a recording of *Masterpiece*, one of my favorite TV shows.

9:30 p.m.: Read a few chapters in *American Hippopotamus,* a quirky book a friend recommended.

10:00 p.m.: Head for bed.

While one day's schedule doesn't show you everything an agent does, it provides you with a peek into a portion. Of course, not every agent has all the same items on her to-do list. That's because some agents actually are failing at their job, as Wendy explains in the next chapter.

CHAPTER 46

#AgentFail: Bad Agents

By Wendy Lawton

Yes, Virginia, there are bad literary agents.

So how does a writer know if an agent is bad? It's a little harder these days than it used to be. We used to tell writers looking for an agent to read the AAR's (Association of Authors' Representatives) *Canon of Ethics*. It spells out how agents are *supposed* to function, basically saying that an agent only makes money from the sale of your work: They only make money when you make money. But even the AAR unofficially admits that the market has changed since the canon was created, with self-publishing and independent publishers muddying the waters. Many agents are having to offer their clients other services, such as helping them create and publish their own product outside of traditional publishers.

But dangers still exist, which is why the canon was established in the first place. Many writers are willing to make huge sacrifices to get published. What a temptation for scam artists. Books have been written about agent scams and editing scams.

One eye-opening one is *Ten Percent of Nothing: The Case of the Literary Agent from Hell* by Jim Fisher, which tells the story of a fake literary agent who bilked writers out of millions of dollars. She never edited the manuscripts as promised, nor showed them to a single legitimate publisher.

But those kinds of scams are less likely than the subtler practices offered today. Here are some suspicious or downright unethical practices:

An Agent Who Wears More Than One Hat

If your agent has a financial interest in an editing firm, a marketing firm or a publishing firm and directs you to those services, he is treading on thin ice. For example, take an agent who gives paid seminars across the country on, say, marketing books overseas. He is totally within the bounds of ethics unless he insists that every one of his clients pay to attend. If an agent takes on clients to feed his other business, it is unethical. An agent might suggest an editor or two who could help you to shape your book, but the decision and financial arrangements have to be up to you. If the agent owned the editing company or were to receive a gift or a kickback for that referral, it is inappropriate. The agent makes money, not by selling your project to a publisher, but by funneling you to an editing company and getting a kickback. It's much easier to make money by sending you to the editing company than by selling your manuscript. It's a conflict of interest.

The same would hold true if the agent offered to edit your manuscript for a fee before submitting it to publishing houses. That would be like your doctor offering to make the medications he prescribes to you, thus making money not only from his medical advice but also from the medicines he's making. His incentive to prescribe expensive—or needless—drugs might be high.

An Agent Who Herds You into Self-Publishing

You have an agent in order to sell your work to traditional publishers. That agent only makes a commission when the publisher pays you an advance or royalties. If he is directing you to self-publishing firms, you need to figure out if he owns an interest or if he is getting a kickback. Of course, many times an agent will need to help a client create product for his own speaking ministry or web store. Or perhaps the agent helps the client create self-published books of out-of-print books. In such cases, the client would pay a pre-agreed commission for this work to the agent.

An Agent Who Poaches Clients

One of the most cringe-worthy practices by marginal agents is wooing successful clients away from their agents. Good agents simply do not do it. If you're already represented and another agent approaches you and talks about your career or makes a pitch to represent you, run the other way! Industry-wide the practice is considered unethical. No matter how flattering it may be, the agent who engages in the tactic will most likely be comfortable with any number of other unethical practices.

You want an agent whose primary mission is to grow your career. But you also need to gauge the actual effectiveness of an agent. You should know:

- Publishing houses to which the agent has recently made sales
- How many sales the agent has made
- Other writers the agent represents

You might wonder where you can get this information. Much of it is available online, such as Publisher's Marketplace or even the agency's own website. Nonetheless, you should ask many of the above questions when an agent offers representation. You should also feel free to talk to some of the agent's clients. If you are already working with an editor, you can ask him indirectly about the agent. Most editors will be uncomfortable giving you a direct yea or nay about whether they like to work with an agent, but if you give him a list of three agents and ask whom he likes to work with, you may get a sense of who is good and who should be omitted from your list. You might also check the website Predators and Editors, and you'll find excellent information on the site Writer Beware.

Who wants to be represented by a scam artist or someone who is over-promising and underperforming? And think of the damage it would do if your agent is one that editors avoid at all costs. Good agents sometimes inadvertently fail, but bad agents can cause havoc.

CHAPTER 47

Working Together

By Janet Kobobel Grant

Now you know that agents have a bunch of rules for what you should and shouldn't do when approaching them. We sound like a bunch of prima donnas:

Don't call me, don't write me, but here are the 2,500 steps to follow in contacting me.

Don't do this, or I'll never respond.

If you think that will convince me to rep you, well, I'm a shark so I won't be taking that bait.

We're not just snippy with people we don't know, either. It occurred to me that it might be enlightening for you to see how sometimes our clients' behavior drives us to distraction.

But first, I want to say I love working with my clients. They're a great group of writers who are laboring away at this creative venture, which seems to require a more dynamic set of skills with each wave of change on an already roiling sea. It takes real guts to *stay* a writer. I'm proud of them for keeping on course, applying their considerable talents to touching others' lives, and remaining steadfast even when they're hit by bad news. But sometimes, I just can't imagine what a certain client was thinking. . .

One of my clients has been a saint in her patience. A publisher offered a contract and sent the contract to me nine months ago. I responded with some pretty aggressive changes I wanted to negotiate. Yet, until last week, that contract hadn't moved beyond the negotiations stage. I made innumerable phone calls, wrote demanding emails, and moved up the publishing house organizational chart to appeal to upper management. But I hadn't budged the contract negotiations. Then, at the end of an inordinate amount of time, I finally received a response to my suggested contract changes. (I had shopped the project elsewhere in the meantime since this wasn't looking promising, but I hadn't landed it with a new publisher yet.) I emailed my client to announce that we were actually moving forward...but she didn't receive my email.

And her patience wore out. She rifled off an email to the editor, in essence saying, "How long do you think I'll wait? I'm beyond frustrated. Cough up the contract. Oh, and I'm attending a conference where you'll be on the faculty. Wanna meet me and explain to me about the delay in person?"

The editor responded that the delay in moving the contract forward was mostly her fault, and yes, she would meet with my client at the conference—and she copied me on the communication, something my client hadn't thought to do.

As I read the interchange between the two, I knew my client had committed a faux pas. She had taken business matters into her own hands and complained to the editor. What did it gain my client? She felt better for saying what she thought. What did she lose? My control of the situation. I had just gone back to the publisher and dug in harder on an issue the publisher didn't want to change in the contract. Now I had a rogue client to deal with. My client's job is to not even acknowledge to anyone at the publishing house that negotiations are going on (or not going on). That gives her the ability to be the author who is just working away at what she does best and not worrying about the business stuff. She gave up our higher ground just when I was pressing in on a very important aspect of the contract, in essence tossing me off the negotiating cliff.

Not only was I distressed at what my client said in her email, but I also was miffed that my client didn't copy me on her important communication with the editor. I don't need to be involved in every little communication between the editor and my client, but I do need to be aware that my client has decided to issue a complaint—and written that communication with an unprofessional tone.

What's the point of my telling you about this mishap? Sometimes an agent's client is the agent's worst enemy, making it hard for the agent to take care of the client. And if your agent can't move the negotiations forward, you won't be able to either.

- **Principle #1 in the author-agent relationship: Never fire off an emotional e-mail to an editor** (or anyone else at a publishing house). If you want to whine, complain, or utter expletives, do it with your agent. I understand how frustrating publishing can be. I've been a writer, I've been an editor, and now I've been an agent for more than 20 years. I grasp how utterly helpless, angry, and frustrated an author can feel. Your agent is a safe place to let off steam. However, anyone else directly connected to the publishing house is unsafe—unlike your agent, that person has a vested interest with the publisher, not with you.
- **Principle #2: Include your agent in conversations of consequence.** In this situation, the editor might develop a strong dislike for my client before they even have a chance to form a working relationship. If my client had mentioned to me that she was going to write such an email, I would have told her not to. If she missed that first stop sign and barreled into the intersection but took me along for the ride (by cc-ing me), I could have joined the conversation and tried to control the damage.

The bottom line in this situation: I was upset not just because my client's actions made my job harder but also because my client made the situation worse for *herself.*

Now, let's discuss how this could have gone differently. I want to commend one of my clients who handled a similar situation in a way that created a win-win situation. She had been trying to arrange with the marketing director at her publishing house a book signing tour, but the marketer wasn't responding. Time was running out to arrange the tour; bookstores were contacting my client begging for details. There were no details to be given. So my client talked to me about the problem, and together we developed a strategy:

- The client would call the marketer's cell phone and leave a message.
- If that didn't bring a response, we would put together a step-by-step process on how to arrange the tour and then inform the marketer what the plan was.
- My client's assistant would follow the plan, taking on the responsibility of overseeing the book tour by making sure bookmarks, books, and giveaways would be at each location. Furthermore, she would communicate with each venue that the author was scheduled to make an appearance.

How did the strategy work out? The marketer finally emailed a response and agreed to the plan we had created.

What a difference from my client who forged ahead without me, communicating inappropriately with an editor. In this case, my client came to me with the problem, and we mutually agreed on a plan and were able to carry it out, with copies of all emails going to both of us. Voila! A seeming conundrum dealt with after weeks of frustration. The ending is a good one because we, in essence, did the marketer's job for her, everyone was brought into the loop, and the book was promoted.

So what can you learn from this scenario?

- **Principle #1: Involve your agent when a problem persists.**
- **Principle #2: Copy all involved individuals on your communications.**
- **Principle #3: Help others do their jobs, when necessary,** especially if it means the difference between a successful promotion plan for your book vs. a failed plan.

CHAPTER 48

Be Open to Your Agent's Perspective

By Janet Kobobel Grant

I spend a lot of my time helping clients to prepare proposals for submission to editors. As I interact with various clients, I have oftentimes observed a similar behavior: Each of us has a preconceived notion about our projects that can make us intractable on certain points. This inability to see a project with fresh eyes can keep us from finding a publisher for our work.

Two cases in point:

1. A client has a stunning idea with much potential. Tied to a key event in our country's history, a book on this topic could make a significant contribution to society's conversation. Yes, really. But the author is convinced a publishing committee will understand the importance of such a book and therefore doesn't need to read the first two chapters of the book that set up the project's importance. Instead, the author insists on submitting chapters starting with Chapter 3. May I just say that I have no confidence in an entire team at a publishing house getting it? My hope is that enough editors will ask for the first chapters to make my point. Wouldn't it just be smarter to write those chapters?

2. Another client has a strong idea for a project, but the competition is stiff. I'm trying to get her to understand that she needs to more tightly focus her idea so it clearly is differentiated from books by well-known authors who have written on the same topic. But she's so intent on *her* perception of the proposal that she can't hear what I'm saying. It's like deciding to open an ice cream shop but refusing to recognize that the three already established ice cream shops in town will present a major roadblock to your success. Maybe you need to add clowns and free balloons to differentiate your shop. Whatever you choose, be smart about it; make your project stand out from a field crowded with celebs.

So what's with this inability to listen? We all have blindsides, but these authors aren't grasping the significant issues I'm pointing out that could make or break their next projects. It's rather like the emperor who has no clothes. Plenty of folks will pretend right along with you that you're regally garbed. And it can be dangerous to point out the, uh, naked truth…but somebody has to do it. And wouldn't you rather it be your agent—or even your mother—than an editor who can choose to not take your project to committee or a publishing committee that gives your project the thumbs down?

If you want to succeed as an author, you have to have a discerning ear: Whom should you listen to? Is it worth forcing yourself to put the brakes on your enthusiasm and refine your project? Or is the "naysayer" wrong, and you should barrel ahead full steam?

I'd say in the two examples I've just given that I'm not asking either writer to rethink an idea, but to think *more thoroughly* about the idea in order to take it to the next level. That's what makes a project one likely to break out—or break into publishing.

CHAPTER 49

Client Mishaps: Kiss of Death

By Wendy Lawton

The phrase *kiss of death* is shorthand for "Uh-oh, that writer has just endangered his or her writing career via something that was done or left undone or done inappropriately." It only takes three words to mark a potential catastrophe. Kiss. Of. Death. And words are not always needed. Janet and I share an eyebrow signal that identifies a kiss of death (KOD) without benefit of words. It works great if the kiss-of-death moment occurs in a crowded room or from a lectern—and doesn't involve one of our clients.

I'm going to choose two potential career killers I've identified as the kiss of death for an author:

The first is the moment an agent receives a call from her client announcing that he has just **quit his day job**. When a writer raises his hand in a workshop to ask a question about an author's remuneration, nine times out of ten he'll hear the old phrase, "Don't quit your day job." Everyone in the room laughs, yet the writer is no closer to uncovering the fiscal realities of his hoped-for avocation. When I was a new writer, it frustrated me. I had come from the world of business and thought it was crazy that no one dealt with the financial realities. Now I understand why.

As financial questions possess so many variables and uncertainties, it is hard to address them in anything other than a one-to-one setting.

And even then, it's impossible to plan. Let's say the book sells to a publishing house. The size of the advance depends entirely on how much competition there was for it, which house bought it, and how much clout the author has. The advance can range from nothing to a million dollars (and sometimes even more!). Statistically, the four-figure advance is much more common than the six-figure advance. Once the book does sell to a publishing house, there's no telling if it will make royalties beyond the advance. Even with a two- or three-book contract, the writer has no guarantee that he will receive another contract after this one is fulfilled unless he has solid, growing sales numbers. And who knows how fast a publisher is willing to offer a contract on any books in the future? Selling the first book guarantees nothing.

Even the multi-published author has to contemplate whether he can afford to quit his day job. It takes a lot of faith, a lot of savings and a lot of courage to live on a writer's income. The mortgage payment comes due every month. So do all the other bills. A writer's money comes in fits and starts—the biggest chunk when the contract is signed, then a designated amount when the publisher accepts the finished manuscript, and sometimes a third amount when the book is published. Royalties of varying but unpredictable amounts hopefully will ensue.

The writer has no control over his income flow. How many writers have turned in a finished manuscript only to have it land on an overburdened editor's desk? As the writer waits impatiently to hear that the manuscript is acceptable, the writer has no idea when this payment will be made. It could be days, weeks, or months from now.

But that's not the only reason an agent hates to hear that a client is thinking of quitting his day job too early. It may seem backwards, but **writing as a second job makes the writer uber-productive**. When you only have a couple of hours a day, those hours are golden. On the other hand, when the whole day stretches out before you, it's easy to lunch with friends, play video games to warm up, and to spend way too much time on social media. Besides that, many writers need to rub shoulders with all types of people in order to write real. The many different people in the work world can provide invaluable inspiration.

The biggest reason quitting a day job can be the kiss of death to authors' careers? **Rather than using their time to write, their energy is focused on trying to keep the money flowing.** The strain of living on a financial roller coaster seems to sap creativity from writers. As the need for money becomes greater, writers often take on too much work, pushing deadlines, working for multiple publishing houses, and rushing the art of writing. To build the kind of career that will allow a writer to eventually write full-time without financial strain, each book has to be better than the last. A writer can't keep chasing deadlines and squeezing in books to make ends meet. He needs freedom to write slowly and artfully.

So that's why, when you announce that you just quit your day job, your agent may look heavenward and whisper the words "kiss of death" under her breath. But does that mean there is never a **right time to become a full-time writer**? No.

The right time to make the career switch to full-time writing can occur when:

- You have multiple contracts.
- Each book you write is selling a little better that the book before.
- You have matched your day job income with writing income.
- You have a good cushion of money in the bank—enough money to cover the mortgage, bills, and expenses for six months.

The second kiss of death can occur through the words you use. In World War II GIs were given four succinct words of advice to keep in mind when writing home, carrying on a conversation, or being captured: loose lips sink ships. I'd like to suggest that loose lips can also be the KOD to a writer's career.

We live in an instant communication age. We email, we blog, we Facebook, we Tweet, we do podcasts, and we create YouTube videos. There are so many different ways we can get ourselves into trouble with a just a keystroke or two. My mother used to caution, "Don't write anything in a letter you'd be embarrassed to see posted on a bulletin board." In this electronic age, I'd have to say the same about any electronic communication: Don't write anything you wouldn't want to see re-tweeted, forwarded, sent to other writers, to your editor, to your agent, to your publishing house, or especially to your mother.

Just last week, I spoke to an editor about one of my clients whose work he's planning to take to committee. He asked me if the client's goals align with those of the publisher. I'd never been asked that before, and I must have hesitated because he went on to explain why he was asking. Apparently, while recently making an offer to an author, someone in his house happened upon a blog post in which that author was sharply critical of the publishing house and its mission. Needless to say, the board withdrew the offer. That opinionated blog turned out to be the kiss of death to that particular partnership.

Did you know that many human resources departments routinely check social networking sites, websites, and follow a potential employee's Twitter stream before making a job offer? Always assume publishing committees also research a potential author. Something said in these public forums has the power to tip the scales.

I cringe when I see authors tweeting negative things about their works-in-progress. Yes, we writers understand the writing process and know that it's normal to hate the book halfway through, but your readers don't know that. What about the writer who blogged about being so glad a certain book was finished? He said it was a mess that he was so sick of he just needed to let it go so he could begin work on the new idea he was passionate about. Hello? How does he think his readers will react to that news? What if his editor or someone from the publishing house reads the blog? Kiss of death.

It's not just written communication that can be a problem. Any kind of talk can get around. When I'm considering a potential client, one of the things I prize is discretion—the ability to always be appropriate. Nothing is more important when trying to build a career, no matter the industry. When I was leading a workshop at a writers conference, someone joked about how many times I used the word *winsome* when talking about how writers need to approach problems. Okay, I admit I overused the word, but it is such an advantage to be pleasing and engaging in an age when snide and snarky are too often the default. Winsome will certainly set you apart. Your mother knew what she was saying when she told you if you can't say something nice, don't say anything at all.

By being aware of these two potential career killers, you can save both yourself and your agent a lot of worry. However, that doesn't mean that agents don't mess up from time to time too.

CHAPTER 50

When the Author-Agent Relationship Isn't Working

By Wendy Lawton

We would all like to think that once we've signed on the representation agreement's dotted line, we would experience a marriage made in heaven. We'll be together forever. But that's not always the case. A number of circumstances can lead to a breakup. Let me just list a few:

- Sometimes **a breakdown in communication** occurs. The client may experience a crisis or need during a time when the agent is away or unable to drop everything. The agent will get a call or an email saying something like, "I just don't feel like we are a good match anymore." Ouch! It always hurts. We agents talk about how we wish we could have anticipated the client's feeling of abandonment.
- Sometimes **the client is approached by another agent** who subtly infers that they could do more. Most reputable agents go out of their way to avoid poaching clients, but it happens. Again, this stings. Unfortunately, it rarely works out well for the client, especially since publishing houses notice writers who agent hop. It rarely sends a positive message.

- Occasionally **a client may decide to take a break** from writing or head off in a different direction. We might keep them on the roster but consider them inactive. Other times we part company and send them off with our blessing. We've been known to touch base from time to time to see if anything has changed.
- Sometimes the agent realizes he has done everything he can think of and still is **unable to get traction for a client**. This kind of failure is hard to swallow, but it's reality. At that point, the kindest thing to do is to let the client go, knowing that perhaps another agent with different contacts may be able to make things happen for the writer. We heard one agent brag at a conference that she's never had a client she couldn't eventually sell. The group of agents who heard this merely coughed politely. Oh, if only that were true.
- Sometimes the client and the agent both realize **the match was simply not a great fit**. When this happens it is a kindness to all concerned to part company.

Thankfully, breaking up doesn't happen often, but nothing is harder than having to say goodbye to all the hopes and dreams we harbored for a talented writer. I've found I've never been able to completely let go. I continue to watch their careers and keep pulling for them to find the success I always believed they could achieve. The antidote for these kind of painful breakups is for both the agent and the author to choose carefully in the first place, to work on communication, and to freely offer kindness to one another.

PART SIX

The Inside Scoop on Contracts and Being Paid for Your Work

CHAPTER 51

The Agent's Contract: What Variables Should You Look for?

By Janet Kobobel Grant

Many variations occur in agencies' representation agreements. One can be one page long, another five.

So what should you look for in an agent's contract?

- **Recognize that agents span the spectrum when it comes to agreements.** Some operate on a handshake (or a nod of the head); others have multi-paged, detailed contracts. Neither is good nor bad. The agent without an agreement is functioning based on publishing conventions and the belief that giving one's word should be sufficient. The second has decided that spelling out how the relationship will work keeps communication on a business level and avoids misunderstandings. The agreement becomes a document both can refer to if the relationship unfolds in unexpected or complicated ways.
- **Understand the term or length of the contract.** Some agencies' agreements specify that they will represent one manuscript. Others want to represent everything you write

in perpetuity. Still others will represent a genre or category of writing, say, children's books. Once again, there is no right or wrong contract. It depends on what works best for you and the agent. Obviously each of these examples is a piecemeal approach to your writing except for the agreement that covers all of your writing. Agencies that are more career-oriented will tend to have that type of contract. It enables the agent to deal with the full scope of your career rather than having to coordinate with another agent or having the author act on his or her own behalf in a different type of writing.

- **Be sure to check how the document specifies the relationship ends**. While each party enters into the agreement with a belief that this will last forever, it doesn't always work out that way. If the agent or author wants to end the relationship, how will that work?

  Some agency contracts specify "at will" endings, which means either the agent or the author may end the relationship at any time. The only caveat is that the agreement is likely to give the agent thirty to sixty days to clear the pipeline, that is, to attempt to collect responses to proposals that editors are considering. So, even after one party gives notice that he or she wants to end the relationship, the agent has that specified number of days to continue working to close out unfinished business. We'll come back in a minute to the issue of what rights agents retain even after the contract is ended.

  However, some contracts tie the author to the agency until a certain number of projects have been written under the agreement. That should raise red flags for you. What if you realize, soon after entering into the relationship, that it isn't what you had hoped? But you are required to produce a number of projects for the agent.

  Signing an agreement that has a set time limit is also a sobering concept for the same reason. If the agreement is for three years, but in the first year you want out...oops, it could be a long wait.

- **Read carefully what rights the agent has to the material he or she places for you.** Most contracts specify that the agent has the right to represent you—and to collect commissions for—any project until the rights are returned from the publisher. That means, if the book is made into a film after you move to another agent, the first agent receives his commission on money you make from the film as well as the boost in royalties that the book will experience. The reason this is the case is that the agent has done the work of finding a publisher for your book and has negotiated the contract. So everything that springs from the book—film, curriculum, audio versions, toys—is under the purview of the agent. No other agent has a right to attempt to sell these subsidiary rights. (The first agent might well work with sub-agents, such as a film agent, in exercising a book's rights. That's a very different matter.)

  Some agents' contracts have a twist to this concept. They state that this agent will have a claim to the commission on any money that book *ever* makes. That means, if the publisher returns the book's rights to the author and a second agent places the book with a new publisher, the first agent receives her commission. The reasoning behind this arrangement is that the book sold well enough at the initial publisher to generate interest from the second publisher, and the first agent was the one who did the work for the title at the beginning of the string of events. While I understand the reasoning, I have to say I don't agree with the concept. Once the rights are returned to the author, unless that writer still is represented by the same agent, it's a whole new game as to what happens to those rights.

Another part of the contract that is also important to pay attention to is how the agent intends to handle your payments, which I've delineated in some detail in the next chapter.

CHAPTER 52

Why Agents Collect Your Money for You

By Janet Kobobel Grant

Literary agencies handle authors' advance payments and royalty payments one of two ways:

1. The money is split—generally 85 percent to you, 15 percent to your agent—at the publishing house.
2. One hundred percent of the money is sent to the agency, where it is split, and the author's sum (85 percent) is sent to him or her.

In my opinion, if your agent isn't doing number 2 for you, he or she is taking the easy way out of providing you a service.

By having the money sent to the agency, that agency will:

- **Know that the money was sent to you.** If the agency receives only its portion, it doesn't know if you got yours. Since the bulk of the funds are the author's, a publisher that's having trouble finding the funds to pay could easily send the 15 percent to the agent but not the 85 percent to the author.
- **Check that the amount sent was correct.** Recently a client's advance payment was sent to our office. But the publisher had failed to send the right amount. Instead, the publisher sent what

it initially offered for the book, not the increased amount I had negotiated. In all likelihood, someone in accounting looked at paperwork that indicated the initial amount offered but failed to check the contract, which stated the increased amount. If the author's money hadn't been sent to me, it would have taken me some time to figure out why the agency's portion was incorrect. But with the entire sum presented in one check, the error was obvious and quickly spotted. And the author didn't happily skip off to the bank to deposit an incorrect check.

- **Double-check that royalty payments are correct.** Reporting royalties and paying the correct amount is a complex business because the book is likely to be published in many formats, at varying discounts, with returns, reserves and licensed subsidiary rights added to the equation. I spend hours poring over royalty statements to determine if the payment for a client is correct. Seeing the sum sent to a Books & Such client is very different from studying a report that only reflects what our agency earned. Spotting errors is hard work, but it's made even harder if the reviewer isn't looking at the total rather than a portion of the total.
- **Make certain the check to the author is made out correctly.** That might seem pretty straightforward, but an agency will be more sensitive to whether an author is incorporated and whether that payment is made out to the author or the author's corporation. When it comes to reporting income to the government, you want the money to be in your corporation's column, not your personal column.
- **Send out 1099 forms to clients rather than having the publisher do so.** Once again, this is a place for the agency to check that the figures on the form are accurate. If the numbers are reported through the publisher, it's up to the author to make sure they're right and to make sure the 1099 is made out to the author or to the corporation, depending on how the author's finances are set up. For the record, the publisher frequently

> makes out our agency's 1099 forms incorrectly, applying them to my Social Security number rather than to the agency's Federal ID number. It becomes our job to correct that with the publisher while we send out a correct 1099 to our client.

Agencies that set up a system in which they receive their commission directly from the publisher don't have the same incentives to check that all is being handled appropriately for the author. And it's much harder to spot the problems, even if the agency looks for them. So, while on the surface it might seem better to have the money headed your way directly from the publisher, in actuality, you're short-circuiting an important aspect of what your agency should be doing for you.

CHAPTER 53

Publishers' Contracts: How Did Contracts Get the Way They Are?

By Janet Kobobel Grant

During my career, I've found myself explaining to a number of clients why some sections of contracts have especially stringent terms. My clients fall silent when I say, "Every paragraph has an author's initials beside it" (which is a quote from an editor, by the way). Those initials are written with invisible ink, but the truth is authors are responsible for much of each publisher's contract.

When I became an agent in 1996, some contracts were three-page visions of elegant simplicity. They covered everything that needed to be agreed to but weren't excessive in demands or so confining that an author had little hope of making a living after signing the document. Today, many contracts are in excess of 25 pages, and it's been a long time since I've seen anything that resembled elegant simplicity. The terms that come to mind are *bloated*, *beyond reason*, and *too complex to comprehend.*

What happened in the intervening years?

Lots of changes, of course. Adequately spelling out the rights in a contract has become a feat worthy of a gold medal gymnast. Digital and multimedia rights alone have added several paragraphs to every contract.

What it means for a book to go out of print has become a complicated matter as well.

But another big factor in fattening up contracts is the authors themselves. Through creative interpretations of the less expansive contracts of old, authors have pushed the line of what they could get away with to limits that astound and shock the unimaginative. To see what they've done is like walking through your house with a burglar as he tells you all the house's vulnerabilities that have never before occurred to you. A publisher, seeing an author violate the publishing house's good will, phones an attorney and asks for new contractual language that protects the publishing house.

Want to know a few of the clauses I'm referring to?

1. If you miss your manuscript deadline, the publisher can cancel the contract—and you must pay back any of the advance given to you in order for the rights to be returned to you. Authors were missing deadlines, sometimes by years, rendering the value of the manuscript less than it was when the publisher offered the advance. These deadlines weren't missed because of family emergencies or unexpected twists in life, but because the author was too busy making money other ways, through speaking venues, public appearances or contracting with other publishers for higher advances and giving the new contract higher priority. Then the authors were asking to acquire the rights back to the incomplete manuscript *and* to keep the advance. If you were the publisher, wouldn't you add protections to your contract?

The result: Missing a book deadline has become much more treacherous. Today, if you miss your deadline and the market has shifted since the contract was signed or your sales numbers have plummeted, the publisher can terminate the contract and get the advance returned. Obviously, the publisher has the choice as to whether to pull the parachute cord, but missing a deadline has become perilous.

2. If the author doesn't pay invoices for copies he bought of the published book, the money can be deducted from any agreement between the publisher and author. Apparently many authors have grieved their publishers by aggressively ordering copies of the published book but failing to pay for those copies. (Authors are offered a special discount in their contracts, encouraging them to purchase copies from the publisher to sell at speaking events or other personal appearances.) As a result, publishers have given themselves the right to dip their hand into any agreement they have with you to deduct from your earnings the money you owe but won't pay. Just picture the scenarios that have occurred to result in every publishing contract having this clause.

3. Noncompetition clauses that result in the author's not being able to produce any book-length work before the last book contracted is published. This has been a deadly clause for authors. Picture this: You sign a three-book contract, agreeing to write one book per year. You're thrilled because you are receiving a nice advance to begin with and then regular payments during the three years you're writing. But, as those years play out, you discover that with such a long time period, the payments aren't adding up to enough for you to remain financially stable. When you check your contract, you find that the noncompetition paragraph locks you into not writing *anything* book-length, regardless of topic or genre, until the third book is *published.*

There are many versions of the noncompetition clause, and I'm portraying it in its most extreme version (which occurs in several publishers' contracts). Publishers are, in essence, locking down authors so the possibility of making a living wage is highly unlikely. Some publishers are immovable when it comes to this clause, but others are willing to make adjustments to it.

How did this paragraph come into existence? Picture the author who decided to contract simultaneously with several publishers and not to inform any of them of the other projects. The publishers, in good faith, invest editorial, marketing and sales dollars (tens of thousands of dollars) into making each book a success—only to discover the author has created competition for him or herself by flooding the market with too many books at once. Everyone loses—each publisher and the author. So the publishers decided to build a fortress around the author, preventing that writer from creating a worst-case scenario. Protection makes complete sense. But now authors who are savvy enough not to cannibalize their own sales must adhere to stringent noncompetes that make it hard to earn a living.

Other examples in contracts abound, but this gives you a taste of the bitter fruit all authors must eat from trees other authors planted. It's not a pretty picture, is it?

Another aspect of the contract that authors care about a lot—and rightly so—is understanding what they will be paid to write the book, which Wendy will address in the next chapter.

CHAPTER 54

The Publisher's Contract: The Money Part

By Wendy Lawton

As agents, we regularly hear three hackles-raising comments from clients regarding the advance an author receives from a traditional publisher. (Remember that an advance is like a loan against future earned royalties that the publisher pays the author to financially assist the writer to be able to write the book.) Those comments are:

- "I need to see at least a xxx-dollar advance for this book."
- "How much of an advance can I expect to get from this book?"
- "I've talked to my friend whose sales are about the same as mine, and she gets xx dollars for her books, but I only get x."

Back when I was first writing, I found it frustrating that I could never find out how much money I could expect to make. I'd sit in writers workshops, but no one would ever ask the question. I've always been a pragmatic sort. I didn't mind paying dues as long as I knew I'd eventually be making x amount of dollars. Is it too much to ask? Who would ever apply for a job and not ask this most basic question?

So why does the first statement, **"I need to see at least a xxx-dollar advance for this book"** raise an agent's eyebrows?

That comment supposes a book is like a product for which the producer sets the price based on the cost of goods, manufacturing, and overhead. That's not how it works in this industry. The money paid to the author of a potential book is set by the market's demand, and we have almost no way of anticipating how strong the demand will be.

If multiple publishing houses are interested in a book, then it goes to auction and the spirited bidding sets the price. The advance may go far beyond what anyone would have normally expected that book to earn out in its first year, but that over-the-top kind of interest may hint at what could happen when the book hits the market.

If only one house is interested, the bean counters at that publishing house go to work and try to figure out how many books they can conservatively expect to sell in the first year (emphasis on *conservative*). They'll offer you that estimated year's royalties as your advance. Barring extenuating circumstances, this could be a take-it-or-leave-it amount, except for a little wiggle room we agents may find to nudge it upward. Those pro forma sales forecasts may be based on what your previous books sold, on what similar books sold, and on the hunches of the sales teams.

Saying you need a certain amount of money for that book makes about as much sense as walking into a Lexus dealership, telling them you need a brand new SUV, and demanding it for $7,000. The arbitrary price has no bearing on reality.

That's also why the question, **"How much of an advance can I expect to get from this book?"** never gets answered until we have an offer in hand. It is largely impossible to forecast. Until we begin to see what kind of interest there is, we would simply be guessing.

I have clients who only clear a four-figure yearly income, others who make a respectable five-figure income, a few who are into six figures, and one who makes seven figures-plus per year. If you asked me to explain why each client receives that amount, it would take forever to answer. The number of variables is staggering—most are out of our control. Success just happens. Or not. We have no idea whether we'll experience riches or poverty, writing-wise. Sad but true.

You might ask what's wrong with the observation, **"I've talked to my**

friend whose sales are about the same as mine. She gets xx dollars for her books and I only get x"?

Isn't that just good market research?

No, on so many levels. First of all, authors can't be compared. There are too many variables and too many subjective issues. Second, talking about contract points with anyone other than your agent is not only inappropriate but also possibly illegal. Many contracts have a nondisclosure clause. Third, many people exaggerate or withhold important details. For instance, some contracts have what are called bonus clauses for performance. For example, if your book hits a specified best-seller list within a specified time after the initial release, an advance bonus is paid to you. You still need to earn back that advance (it is a loan, after all), just as you must earn back your original advance before you receive royalties. And bonuses are hard to reach; they're seldom ever paid.

Yet I've often heard agents or writers add the bonus to the advance to come up with a much heftier number for reporting. When I hear a number thrown out by an author, I'm always skeptical.

Advances are just one part of the picture. Some best-selling authors would rather trade big advances for higher royalties since they make far more in the long run. Others go for broke and take a reduced royalty to get a bigger advance. A writer who tries to line himself up to another writer's yardstick is probably comparing apples to oranges.

Many of the questions that repeatedly come up wherever writers gather contain the word *average*. What is the average advance a [fill in the genre] writer can expect these days? What is an average print run? What is an average first year sales figure for a [fill in the genre] book? What is the average amount of time from query to contract?

I hear what the writer is trying to get at in each one of those questions, but if he or she were to get an exact answer, it would be worse than meaningless—knowing the average is often dangerous. It leads to faulty expectations.

Let's take the average advance for a first-time book. Some writers who are publishing with smaller publishers receive no money at all. Many small presses pay a modest stipend like $1,000. A few debut books have gone as high as a million dollars at auction. So would that mean an average advance is $1,001,000 divided by three?

If so, the average advance for a first-time book would be $333,667.

Okay, not enough samples. So how does anyone go about getting enough samples? Advance figures are confidential. Do a Google search for average book advance—you'll see all kinds of silly suppositions. Any number given will be meaningless because (a) there is no way to get the data to do a reliable average, (b) no two books are the same (Some have much more commercial appeal; others, less.), and (c) no two authors are the same. Some would prefer to take a more modest advance and collect their money on the backend.

Picture a number axis stretching from zero to one million. If the average were to be verified to be, say, $5,000, would that help? Only with comparisons and making an author either swell with pride or feel diminished. Your advance could come anywhere on that axis so what good would it be to know an average?

The question the writer is really asking is, "What kind of advance can I expect?" It's certainly a question for your agent, and he or she can *guess*, but there is no way of knowing until the manuscript is sent to publishers and interest is gauged. If multiple publishers are interested, there's no telling where the price might go.

The important question is this: What is the royalty percentage? Happily, the advance, while a loan, doesn't need to be paid back if the book doesn't earn out. But that also means the author won't see any future royalty payments above and beyond that advance until the book has sold enough copies to earn back the advance. Once that happens, the author begins to get checks from the publisher every three months or six months.

So, what kind of royalty rate can I expect? Some publishing houses figure royalties based on the cover price of a book, and some publishers base their royalty rate on the net price or price for which the books was sold. The royalties are adjusted appropriately.

For instance, if you had a $10.00 retail price on a book, one publisher might give you 8 percent of the cover price while another would give you 15 percent of the net price. Since most publishers sell to stores with a 40 percent discount, that 15 percent would net close to the same amount as the 8 percent cover price, considering that the publisher paying on net may sell a few books at discount. To complicate things further, your agent may negotiate escalations, meaning that you may get 15 percent on the first 10,000 books sold, then 17 percent on the next 10,000 books sold, and finally 19 percent thereafter. And remember, those are typical percentages. Your contract may offer less, or you may get slightly more—it all depends on the strength of the book.

Here's the truth—there are no average advances. There are no average sales. There are no average books. Best of all, there are no average writers. All we can do as agents is get the work out there and let the market dictate value. The publisher works hard to try to anticipate sales, but the best he or she can do is follow his or her gut. And a writer can only write the best book possible and put it out there.

PART SEVEN

The Inside Scoop on What Happens after Your Book Is Contracted

CHAPTER 55

The Publishing Relationship: An Overview

By Janet Kobobel Grant

Once your contract is signed, your relationship with your publisher remains at arm's length until you turn in your manuscript to your editor. From there:

- **The production schedule is put in place.** A product manager will determine a schedule for each element in the production process: editorial, design, typesetting (or formatting an e-book), and finally the printer date and the book's release date. The process is more involved for print books because the print buyer has to order the right paper in quantity for other books as well as yours to get the best price.
- **The editorial process begins.** Your book will be seen by a variety of editors. Those roles are explained in Chapter 61.
- **The book is designed.** The designer begins work on the cover and interior layout of your book as soon as your manuscript is received. He or she is given an overview of your book's subject and genre in initial meetings with the acquisitions editor and

the content editor. The designer will translate all the input into design proofs. He'll present these in the next meeting with acquisitions, editorial, the marketing manager, and a sales person until they narrow down to one or two choices. They might send you their final choice, or you might have the opportunity to see the top contenders. Your input generally is sought on the cover, but the publisher contractually has the final say.

- **The marketing department creates a marketing plan to spread the word about your book.** (See Chapter 57, "Relating to the Marketing Team," for more details.)
- **The sales team is introduced to your book at a sales conference.** Usually your book's editor talks to the team about the book and its highlights as well as tells them about you. Sometimes the head of marketing makes this presentation. Either way, not only is your book introduced to the team, but specifics about you as the author and how you'll help to promote your book are discussed as well.

That's an overview of the book-making process. It's much more complex, with lots of other players involved, but those are the broad strokes of how a manuscript becomes a book.

CHAPTER 56

The Editor: Your In-House Advocate

By Janet Kobobel Grant

You might not realize it, but your editor is also the manager of your project. Every step of the publishing process is overseen by your editor. (Generally we're talking here about the editor who acquired your book; sometimes this person will also be the individual who edits your book.

Your editor is your in-house advocate. If the creative staff come up with a cover you don't like, your editor is the in-house person who speaks on your behalf. If the title is, in your opinion, all wrong, it's your editor who conveys that thought to everyone else involved in the packaging process.

Your editor not only troubleshoots areas you might not be pleased with in the book's development, but also offers his or her opinions on cover, back cover copy, title, interior design, and font. When I was an in-house editor, I was the person who initially made title and cover suggestions to the graphic designers, and sometimes I rewrote marketing's back cover copy and catalog copy. Now, at some houses, editors aren't allowed that kind of leeway, but no one at the publishing house knows your project better than the editor—and no one has as close of a relationship with the author as the editor.

In addition to these tasks, the editor often (this will vary from publishing house to publishing house) is simultaneously:

- acquiring new projects;
- reading potential proposals and manuscripts;
- traveling to writers conferences;
- meeting with key authors to brainstorm ideas;
- editing at least one manuscript but probably more;
- attending brainstorming sessions on titles;
- giving input on cover designs;
- looking at catalog copy;
- reading back cover copy;
- attending the requisite business meetings; and
- presenting projects to the editorial committee, the publishing committee, and often the sales reps in hopes of getting approval to offer a contract.

So if your editor doesn't answer your phone calls right away or takes a while to give you feedback on your revised manuscript, you can see why. Today's editor is stretched thin.

CHAPTER 57

Relating to the Marketing Team

By Janet Kobobel Grant

Once your manuscript is close to being edited, you're likely to receive an email from the marketing director, introducing you to those who will be working on getting the word out about your book: the marketer (who will buy social media ads, oversee the creation of any in-store material that will advertise your book and, most importantly, who will have a budget to work with) and the publicist (who gets you that gig on Oprah—or your local radio—and doesn't have a budget).

At this point, the marketing team might send you a marketing plan. If it doesn't, have your agent ask if the two of you can see it. Your agent will help you to understand what the various parts of it mean and what level of marketing you're being given.

You'll periodically hear from the marketing staff as they need you to do such things as write an article for a significant blog or online magazine, plan to post online memes that they've created for you, or other marketing strategies.

However, they'll expect you to do some marketing as well. Letting them know what you plan and what you're actually doing is imperative.

One of my clients learned this the hard way. This was a new client for me, but she had published five books with the publisher who now was producing her sixth title. I asked the editor and the head of marketing what the in-house perception was of my client's marketing skills. They thought she was ineffective.

I then asked the author what she had done to promote her last book. Wow, her list was impressive. From calling on local bookstores and asking them to carry her book to online zany book contests that brought a fantastic response, my client was out there, working every marketing angle I could think of.

"Sandy," I asked, "how much of what you did was communicated to the marketing team?"

"Well, none I guess," she responded. "I just thought they'd check my blog, my website, and my social media and see what I was doing."

A publishing team doesn't have time to regularly check what each author is doing to promote his or her book.

I gave Sandy an assignment: Every week, just drop a friendly email to her editor, the marketer, and the publicist, listing (no paragraphs with tons to read, but a list the reader could just scan) everything she had done in the past week to market her book.

What a change occurred in her relationship with everyone at the publishing house! The publisher is no longer grumbling that Sandy doesn't contribute to the marketing of her books. Instead, the publisher is stepping up what it is doing *for* Sandy because the publishing team realizes she's investing plenty of her own time and money.

So what's the lesson to be learned from my client? *You* are the most important participant in your marketing. Put together a marketing plan for your next book and *tell your publisher what that plan is.* Then go for it! (More about marketing your book appears in Part 8, "The Inside Scoop on Marketing Strategies That Will Sell Copies of Your Book," beginning with Chapter 66.)

CHAPTER 58

You and Your Publisher: New Best Friends? Not!

By Janet Kobobel Grant

Once a writer signs a publishing contract, everyone involved is dizzy with happiness. The editor, the marketing people, the sales reps, the author, and the agent are all like teenagers who have just met someone new who looks to be on the path to becoming your best friend. The future looks positively, giddily full of promise.

That perception is right...almost. The folks at the publishing house are not your new best friends...they're your new best colleagues. If everyone acts like a BFF, eventually the truth of the relationship will surface, and disappointment or even a sense of betrayal could result.

To approach these relationships with appropriate professionalism, follow these tips:

- **Do not assume that what you say to one person stays with that person.** Everyone at the publishing house works daily with everyone else. Okay, that seems obvious, but think about the repercussions of, say, complaining to your editor that the person who wrote your back cover copy is lame-brained or that she didn't bother to even read your book! That might be the individual the editor has lunch with almost every day.

- **Do not deride any other books your publisher has chosen to produce.** Okay, so you think some very-famous-but-can't-write-his-way-out-of-a-paper-bag author shouldn't have been given the chance to show off his lack of skills–let alone have a mega marketing budget. Here's the thing: That author might well be providing the infusion of cash the publisher needs to produce your book and to pay employees' salaries. Zipped lips also apply to books on politics, religion, or social justice that the publisher produces. Your negative opinion about any of those books isn't sought or desired.
- **Do not confess that you don't read any books within the genre in which you write.** You have just proclaimed that you're writing with blinders on—that you don't even particularly like your genre. Especially if you admit this to your editor, red flags will start snapping in the wind for her. And she'll start to worry. If you don't know the rules for your genre, how then can you produce the best manuscript? Just how much work will she have to do to pull you from the brink of disaster? (By the way, if you want to be a professional, read a lot of books in your genre—but not while you're writing your manuscript. You could inadvertently start to borrow ideas from other authors.)
- **Do not assume your publishing house will understand that you missed your deadline** because you received a bigger advance for another project at a different publisher after signing a contract with this house. This is not a family affair; you have acted unprofessionally and quite likely breached your contract.
- **Do not divulge that your wild weekend left you debilitated** on Monday and unable to work. Sure, you think the person you're talking to on the phone or writing an email to might have experienced a similar weekend. But you don't know. And just because they did doesn't mean it's okay for you to have

gone and done likewise. That individual might be offended—and that surely can't do your image any good. Unless, of course, your book is about what a bad boy or girl you are.

- **If you have missed your deadline, don't publicly display that you're procrastinating** by spending hours commenting on Facebook posts or tweeting endlessly. The good folks at the publishing house are connected to you via social media.

If some of these scenarios seem far-fetched, I assure you they are not.

Other ways in which you could be reminded that this is a business relationship, not a personal one include the following:

- When the editor tells you that the manuscript must be rewritten.
- When the publisher asks you to pay back the advance because you breached the contract.
- When you dislike the title or cover design chosen for your book, but Barnes & Noble has based the number of copies it will order on both remaining as is.
- When the marketing manager doesn't return your phone calls or respond to your emails because he doesn't want to explain to you how small your marketing budget is.
- When the editor you worked with so well is assigned to edit Famous Author #1's books rather than yours.

Ultimately, remember this: You have entered into a professional relationship. And while writing is a highly personal experience and many people at the publishing house will learn lots about you as they work with you, every one of them will *always* protect the publishing house over you. Always. That's their job.

CHAPTER 59

How to Avoid Deadline Disaster

By Wendy Lawton

Once the contract is signed, you're likely to solemnly realize a publisher actually expects you to complete your manuscript by a date you committed to in writing. As you face the deadline, you might well kick yourself for wishful thinking. You know. . .the editor asked if you could possibly get the book done in six months instead of eight months and in the Sally-Field-like euphoria of the moment ("They like me, they really, really like me!"), you said, "Sure." Now you realize you are in the first third of the book. You hate your characters. The book is stupid. The setting seems inane. You spend more time playing the latest video game craze than working on the manuscript. And the deadline looms in just ten weeks. Gulp!

How does deadline disaster happen so often?

- When we are trying to set a realistic deadline for an upcoming book, we are often in the final stages of our current book. That's when the writing begins to flow. We know our characters. All the plot threads are coming together, and the words are flying off our fingers. When I was actively writing, I'd get so excited about the possibilities during that golden time. I could average 5,000 words a day with gusts up to 7,500. I'd start plotting and planning how quickly I could write a book given those numbers. Duh! Writing speed needs to be averaged over the whole book—the excruciatingly slow first part of the book, the draggy middle, and the sizzling final portion.

- We didn't factor in ramp time. Every time you leave a project, you need to plan on extra time to get ramped up to speed again. We have mini-ramp time with every new day. More ramp time on Mondays. Serious ramp time after an extended time away from the project.
- We tend to be optimists, best-case-scenario planners. Unfortunately, things happen. A child gets sick. An aging parent needs care. A spouse loses his job and is at home all day. We injure a tendon in our typing hand. We lose a loved one and find we can barely write our names let alone write a compelling book. If we've allowed no time in the schedule for unforeseen events, we are tempting fate.
- We need to make money, and writing faster may seem like the best way to accomplish more funds in a shorter span of time. But each writer can only produce so much output per day. Needing money doesn't result in amping up productivity.
- Sometimes we are just too new at this and don't yet understand our own creative rhythms. When an editor asks, "Can you do this in six months?" you figure he wouldn't ask if it weren't possible.
- Some of us are people pleasers. Remember the song from Oklahoma? "I'm jest a girl who cain't say no. . ."?
- We don't factor in time for the book to rest before we begin rewriting and smoothing the book out. Any writer who thinks he can turn in a first draft will not be seeing future contracts. Editors are demanding cleaner and better manuscripts all the time. Allow space in your writing schedule to do sufficient rewrites.
- We also don't figure in enough time for our first readers to read the manuscript and get it back to us.

What can you do to avoid deadline panic?

- Keep accurate daily records of your writing progress. After a few books you'll have a good idea of your own pattern of writing.
- Keep a list of unplanned things that cropped up during each book. Doctor visits, vacations, that broken ankle—all of it. You'll never be able to factor all this into your future planning, but it will remind you that life is messy and that you can expect some surprise time stealers during the writing of that next book.
- Don't give an answer to an editor's request for deadline possibilities off the top of your head. Think about it. Talk to your agent. Be realistic.

For the person who is not yet contracted, how can you prepare for the question of how much time it takes you to write a book?

- So many not-yet-published writers say, "I wish I had a deadline. I'd write much better to a deadline." How do you know? You need to give yourself a deadline and then keep track of your progress just as a contracted writer would. This information will be invaluable when you are contracted.
- If you have critique partners, ask them to act like editors and hold you to your deadlines. No excuses.
- If you find you can't write under those conditions, you'll know writing for publication is not for you. You'll save yourself years of angst. Or, you know you'll need to write a complete manuscript before you seek a contract—maybe through your entire writing career.

One Books & Such client always turns in her manuscripts early to editors. She says she creates a schedule *mathematically*: "Say I have a 12-chapter nonfiction book that is due in 12 weeks. First, I subtract two weeks of slack for unforeseen illness or family emergencies. Then I divide the number of chapters into those remaining weeks. So, in that case, because I'd already written the first two chapters, I'd have to complete one chapter each of the next 10 weeks by SATURDAY. If I haven't, I do NOT allow myself any fun—no meals out with friends, no extended phone calls, no TV." You get the idea. No fun if the chapter's not done. Just do the math—and stick with the schedule.

But what happens when you commit to a deadline by signing the contract and then miss it? What are the repercussions?

CHAPTER 60

How to Avoid Deadline Disaster: Uber-Late Deadlines

By Janet Kobobel Grant

Let's say you missed your book deadline not by a few days, not by a few weeks, but by a few months…or years. If you're seriously late, a whole host of departments in the publishing house pay the price for your missed deadline. And so do you.

- The book won't receive the editorial attention that would make it a better book.
- Marketing will have to scuttle the marketing/publicity plan because the book is no longer coming out in the season it was scheduled for. Your book's marketing dollars have been spent and can't be retrieved. So your book now has no marketing budget left for when it really releases.
- Bookstores have placed orders, but now the publisher's sales reps have to explain that the book will release later. The sales reps' efforts are lost. The bookstore's decision to buy your book proved to be a bad choice (and the bookstore's buyer will remember that you can't make your deadlines).

See the ripple effect? It's not pretty.

If you end up writing the book of the century…too bad, the publisher and the book buyers won't be able to gear up for the big burst necessary to get your stunning book noticed.

The ultimate losers? The publisher, who becomes less and less likely to garner enough sales on the project to make a profit (and who has been carrying the first portion of your advance as a loan to you); the bookstore buyer, who took a chance on ordering your book but learned not to do that again; and you, who fell out of favor with the publisher and everyone employed therein.

I remember receiving an email from one of my clients who was late, late, late on a deadline. He told me he was currently vacationing in Paris, sipping an espresso, and pondering his manuscript—but not actually working on it. Know who else got this email? Several individuals at his publishing house whose jobs would be more secure if the author would come through with what is supposed to be an important book. I understand that the author was assuaging his guilty conscience with the missive, but the communication did more damage than it did damage control.

Life happens to everyone, including authors. Sometimes illness, moving to a new location, writer's block, and accidents interfere with the best-laid plans to complete a manuscript on time. That's not what we're talking about here.

I'm thinking about the authors who have lunch with their friends, blog and tweet endlessly, take vacations, make sure their houses or gardens are pristine, but yet never manage to have time to work on their manuscripts until a couple of weeks before the due date. Then, it's a mad dash to the deadline, which often is missed. And the work is lower quality than it could have been.

I wish this *modus operandi* were unusual, but it's not. I recall one publisher saying to me, "What really kills me is when an author is late on a deadline, but every blog I read has a comment from that person, or they're commenting in all kinds of online professional conversations. I'm thinking, if you just wrote that number of words on your manuscript, you'd be that much closer to handing it in."

Yeah, everyone at the publisher's notices if an author is showing up online but no manuscript is showing up at the publishing house.

I can only conclude three reasons, from my observations, as to why deadlines are seriously missed:

- **Procrastination** is a common ailment among writers. Any activity is more appealing than putting BIC (Butt in Chair) and actually working on the manuscript.
- **Authors are inherently optimistic** (and sometimes unrealistic) when they commit to a deadline when signing their contract (see Wendy's chapter 59).
- **Advances have lost their meaning among authors.** Why did advances come into existence? So authors would have sufficient money to set aside other financial pursuits, enabling the writer to concentrate on writing the book contracted. If the author can't meet his deadline, why does he think the publisher should pay him an advance for his next book? Or even offer him another contract?

Well, publishers are asking themselves that very question. As a matter of fact, a number of publishers have remembered that their contracts enable them to cancel publishing a book if the author misses the deadline. So some authors are receiving a nasty surprise when they turn in their late manuscript. The publisher says, "No thanks—and give me back the portion of the advance I paid you."

Considering all that is lost when a book is uber-late, the publisher's decision is hardly a surprise.

Next, I'll discuss what to expect when your manuscript goes to the editor.

CHAPTER 61

What's It Like to Have Your Manuscript Edited?

By Janet Kobobel Grant

Once your contract is signed, it's time to establish a working relationship with the person who will be your content editor.

- Here are a few protocol items to keep in mind as you dip into working with the staff at the publishing house: Find out how your editor likes to work. How involved does he or she want to be in the process as you write? Some editors want to see the work as it's progressing to provide you with guidance along the way. Other editors are available to answer specific questions while you're writing such as whether you need to get permission to quote a song lyric or how you legally handle telling events from other people's lives in the book. This second type of editor wants to wait until you hand in your manuscript before reading or giving feedback on the writing.
- Keep in mind that several individuals will have a hand in readying your content for publication. Here, in a glance, are those people:

- The acquisitions editor is the person the agent submitted your proposal to. This is the individual who took your project to the various publishing committees and presented to the committees why a contract should be offered. This also is the individual with whom your agent most likely negotiated the basics of the offer.
- Sometimes this is also the editor who will do what is called the substantive or content edit. The manuscript's structure, logic, and—for novels, character development and dialogue—and other broad issues are dealt with by the substantive editor.
- The next person to work on your manuscript is the line or copy editor. This person digs into the details of the manuscript—punctuation, grammar, endnotes, tightening the writing, etc.
- Your manuscript will receive at least one round of proofreading, often completed by a freelance proofreader.
- Sometimes all the editorial work will be completed by freelance workers; sometimes a mix of freelance and in-house personnel will be employed; and for other publishing houses, all the work is done in-house.

- Other steps your manuscript will go through include:
    - Fiction: Review letter and comments in manuscript by substantive editor.
    - Fiction: Rewrite (at least once).
    - Author reviews the edits at least once in the process, sometimes after each edit.
    - Galleys read by proofreader or editor and by author.
- Understand there are different people for different issues. At times you may work with a line editor, other times an author relations manager, and sometimes someone in marketing.
- Make sure not to copy everyone in the publishing house with every bit of news or every question. Most emails should be

directed to one person. Every time you add another recipient, you complicate things in house: Who is responsible to reply? Do all the recipients need to coordinate?

- Never tackle problems with your publisher on your own. Let your agent handle any potential thorny issues.

CHAPTER 62

Extra! Extra! Author Dies While Reading Edited Manuscript!

By Janet Kobobel Grant

Most editors are conscientious about not violating an author's creative efforts but instead strive to clarify and elucidate through any changes made.

But what if, when you read your edited manuscript, you're confused, frustrated, or downright upset by some changes?

I've been on both sides of this fence. I can still recall a conversation with an author I had decades ago about changes I'd made in his manuscript. Our phone conversation began with his telling me the comma corrections I had made in the first sentence should not have been made. I pointed out the sentence had been punctuated incorrectly. He didn't believe me. I told him I would find the punctuation rule in a grammar book and send the reference to him. He still wasn't convinced, and I decided we had better move on to the more substantial changes I had made in the manuscript.

Instead, however, he moved on to the second sentence of the manuscript, in which I had made another minor change. I explained the grammatical rule that had been violated in his writing. Once again he was unimpressed.

That's when I realized he was going to challenge every jot and tittle that had been edited. So I decided to bring a bit of reality into the situation. I asked, "Do you believe your manuscript is perfect, without flaw?"

"Yes," he replied.

The book never was published because he wouldn't allow any changes to the manuscript, despite its actually needing a pretty aggressive editorial hand.

I've also been on the other side of the fence as the author. When I received the edited manuscript for one of my books, I was so appalled by the severity of the edit that I crawled into bed and stayed there for two days. I couldn't figure out how to approach the editor with such a long list of changes with which I disagreed.

So what's an author to do, if you feel wronged by the editing process? Start out by knowing your rights.

Most contracts specify what is appropriate for a publishing house to change. Here's some typical wording: "The Publisher shall have the right to edit and revise the manuscript; provided, however, that such editing or revision shall not materially change the meaning, or materially alter the text of said Work without the Author's consent. Editing to correct infelicities of expression, misstatements of fact, misquotations, errors in grammar, sentence structure, and spelling, and editing to make the Work conform to the Publisher's style of punctuation, capitalization, and like details shall not be considered materially changing the manuscript."

Okay, so we have guidelines as to what is an appropriate change and what isn't. The author who didn't think I should change the punctuation and grammatical errors in his manuscript was operating outside the boundaries he had agreed to when he signed the contract.

On the other hand, the editor of my manuscript had added several examples to illustrate points. If I didn't agree to those additions, I contractually had a right to say I wanted them removed.

What did I do? I remembered what I, in my role as an editor, had often told authors who questioned why I had made a certain change. "I made the change for a reason. If you don't like the way I changed it, let's talk about why I made it. I'm very open to seeing an alternate way to solve the problem I found."

In that spirit, I went to work on reinstating my sense that this was my manuscript and talking with the editor about how to make the manuscript all it could be. Like any good negotiation, some things didn't go the way I wanted; other times the editor gave in despite disagreeing with me. I didn't die from the malady called "the editing process" because we were able to openly communicate and discuss what would work best.

I might suggest you enter into an unemotional conversation with the editor about why changes were made and how to retain your voice in the manuscript. Of course, it's not always so easy to know when an editor has overstepped those boundaries.

Here are a few guidelines that help the writer who can't see clearly what is improved and what is over-edited:

- Has the editor rewritten rather than edited? If an editor adds his illustration, that is overstepping. If your nonfiction book needs an illustration, the editor should ask you to provide one, not provide one for you.
- Words that aren't part of your vocabulary are inserted. Remember that every change the editor makes likely pinpoints a problem in your manuscript. Maybe you used the same word too often. Maybe the word you chose wasn't quite right. Find out why the change was made and adjust the sentence accordingly.
- The editor made adjustments that change what you intended to say. Sometimes an editor guesses wrong about what you were trying to communicate. Even if the correction changes your intended meaning, the editing points out that you weren't clear.

If you want to convince your editor to relent:

- Present your reasons without emotion ("I just feel it's right" won't work).
- Solicit feedback from potential readers. I'm not talking about your friends and family here. Instead, ask your critique group or your agent or take an informal survey from those who are in the appropriate age group.

- Choose your battles. You can't ask the editor to rethink 75 percent of the editing she's done. Decide which edits are so important that you want to resist them.
- Recognize that you want a long-term relationship with the publishing house and with the editor. Be a team player, and the editor is likely to respond in kind.

Next, you need to know when to relinquish your opinion. You've gone back and talked over the changes with your editor, but the two of you are at loggerheads over some issues. You're sure you're right, and the editor's confident she's right. I'd suggest that you ask for neutral, but professional, feedback. That would be your agent. Your agent's job isn't to work through each and every nitpicking change the editor made but to discuss with you the more sweeping adjustments. Because agents read many manuscripts and often have been editors, they can bring perspective and help to discern what editorial changes are puzzling.

One of my clients was sure her manuscript needed to end a certain way. But the editor thought that ending wasn't resounding and had her own idea about the conclusion. No amount of conversation seemed to move either party.

So, I read the two endings and realized the editor was right. I explained to my client why I, as a reader, preferred the one ending over the other. My client was reticent to agree.

So finally, I said, "The publishing house has invested a lot of money in your manuscript, and everyone there wants the book to be a huge success. All those of that professional team who have read the edited version of the manuscript like the ending. If I bought this book, I would find the ending satisfying. Not one of us wants an inadequate conclusion. So, ultimately, you need to trust our opinion."

The author agreed. The book comes out next year, and I'm willing to bet that once she receives good reviews as well as letters and emails from readers who loved the book, she'll decide the edited ending must have been okay.

Those dynamics occur when you're working with an editor assigned to you by the publisher, but how does the author-editor relationship work when you're self-publishing and have hired an editor?

CHAPTER 63

Self-Publishing and Editing

By Janet Kobobel Grant

I've written a number of books, and I seldom looked at an editor's work on my manuscript and felt good about what I saw. I took umbrage when I would note words changed, sentences rearranged, and darlings murdered—yes, murdered.

Looking back, I realize I was hypersensitive, and my work generally was served well by the editors. But some self-published writers bypass them or unwittingly hire freelance editors who aren't especially experienced or skilled.

I don't think hiring someone who cleans up your spelling, grammar, and punctuation is the same as letting your work be scrutinized by a capable substantive editor. Such an editor looks to see if the work flows well and has strong structure, if the theme threads well through the manuscript, if transitions are in place, if the voice remains true or whether the reader is jarred by a voice shift, if details are unclear, if permissions and releases have been acquired, if the best words are put to their correct use, if the author has a penchant to overuse certain words or sentence structure, if the beginning is intriguing, if the ending is satisfying, and if the middle sustains the reader's interest.

There is no substitute for an editor with a good eye and a strong sensibility for what a manuscript can be.

A few weeks ago I launched into a novel I had been eager to read. But by the time I had reached page ten, I was wondering if it would be presumptuous for me to write an email to the acquisitions editor (to whom I've sold a number of projects) to gently mention the three glaring grammatical errors that tweaked my nose out of shape and interrupted my appreciation of the book: the word *unique* with a modifier, a dangling modifier that changed the meaning of a sentence, and a misused noun.

I know not everyone would find those errors worthy of writing an email, but haven't you read a book and wondered how the editor could have allowed the shambles of that manuscript to be typeset?

That lack of editorial skill and oversight doesn't occur just in publishing houses, but also among freelance editors. But here's the catch: Many individuals who have had a couple of books published have declared themselves freelance editors. Being an author does not necessarily qualify someone to be an editor. Those people have two different skill sets. I can edit a novel, but I don't think I could ever write a good one.

Buyer beware! Don't just accept that someone is a skilled editor because he or she has been successfully published or because someone teaches English. Here are a few questions you could ask to determine how adept a person is at editing:

- What editing training have you received?
- What courses have you taken that taught you to edit?
- Who has mentored you in editing?
- What books on editing have you studied?

Before you invest in an editor, take a moment to ask questions that go beyond, "What projects have you edited?" Because some publishers no longer have in-house editors, they rely on freelancers. That means even those with less than stellar skills can show you a list of their achievements.

We've covered publishing relationships, deadlines, and editing so far in this section, but in the next chapter, we'll turn our attention to the times in a writer's career in which he or she must wait—to hear from an agent, to obtain a contract, to hold tight until the publisher releases his or her book. How can a writer productively use those pauses?

CHAPTER 64

In the Meantime... Perfect Your Craft

By Wendy Lawton

What is an author to do once he or she has finished the book, circulated queries and proposals, and is now in an interminable wait?

The longer the wait, the more time we have for self-doubt and second-guessing. That's counter-productive. If you are serious about becoming a career writer, now is the time to be proactive. Once your book is contracted and you are on your way, you will find yourself carried along on a whirlwind. You'll be writing the third book, doing edits for the second book, looking at the page proofs for the first book and planning a marketing push for your debut. **Never again will you have this gift of time**. You need to proceed with confidence and use this waiting period to set up your infrastructure, build an inventory of manuscripts, connect with colleagues, perfect your craft, and pre-market yourself.

Seeking to be become a published author is the grandfather of all waits. The good news is that there's plenty you can accomplish during the wait. Let me just highlight a few things:

- **Hone your craft**: Lavish time on a manuscript. Learn everything you can now and enjoy writing sans pressure.

- **Build your network of peers**: This is the time to get to know other writers. These are the people who will help influence and endorse your books and commiserate with you along the journey.
- **Gather your tribe**: You have no readers until your book is out there, but identifying your readers and hanging out with them online is one of the best things you can do. If you are writing, say, in the field of productivity, find the blogs and networks where productivity aficionados hang out. Participate. Give much more than you receive. It's all part of earning a readership.
- **Learn to harness technology**: How I wish I had learned to build a website and mastered every feature in Photoshop before my life got so crazy busy. Now is a time when you can seriously learn to use the tools you'll need in a digital age.
- **Create a unique social network persona**: Spend time online. With your book and brand in mind, become memorable. Gain a significant following by offering valuable content. These days, nothing outside of a knock-'em-dead book will help you to get published faster than if you are the go-to blogger on a subject that connects to your book. By go-to blogger I mean the name everyone thinks of when your subject comes up.
- **Develop your website**: Your online base. This is as important to your business as a compelling storefront used to be to a retail establishment. Be innovative and always keep your reader in mind.
- **Meet editors and agents**: This is a significant part of the professional network you are building. Where do you accomplish this? At writers conferences. Online. I see many writers connecting in a meaningful, appropriate way to agents and editors on Facebook and other social media. Never has it been easier to get to know professionals.

If I could give you one more piece of advice, it would be to move forward with confidence. Plan for success and use the gift of time. Henry David Thoreau said it better: "If one advances confidently in the direction of one's dreams, and endeavors to live the life which one has imagined, one will meet with a success unexpected in common hours."

CHAPTER 65

Make the Most of Being a Noncelebrity Author

By Janet Kobobel Grant

One of my clients sent me a *Reader's Digest* humorous article entitled, "I'm a Non-Celebrity—Buy My Book." The author, Mike Reiss, is a children's writer who finds his books competing for shelf space with Queen Latifah, Queen Rania of Jordan and Sarah Ferguson among many other famous folks. His conclusion: He's fighting for attention against two queens and a duchess. And, because of the alphabetizing of books by authors' names, his titles rest on bookstore shelves between stories by Carl Reiner and Leann Rimes.

Why, he bemoans, does everyone have to write children's books?

Don't you just know how he feels? While new authors are working their hearts out to be noticed, and mid-list authors wonder how they'll ever get out of the neutral zone and into the noticed zone, publishers are eager to sign up all the usual suspects for yet another rewinding of the same basic material they've been publishing for years. It gives "there's nothing new under the sun" a whole new meaning.

Not that the best-selling author didn't work hard to get there and doesn't continue to work hard. Most do.

But some come by success easily and hold onto it loosely. Success isn't always a gift when it comes to developing character or the writing craft. But, hey, we all know life isn't just or simple to understand; it's complicated.

So what did Mr. Reiss do in the face of every celebrity in the world having a children's book to add to his or her list of accomplishments? He chose to look at the upside to the trend.

One day he received a phone call from a publisher. Not to ask if Reiss would publish one of his children's books with them, but to explain that they had a contract with an African American superstar whose manuscript was unusable, even by celebrity standards.

"They asked me—a Jewish kid from suburban Connecticut—to write a book about growing up as a poor black kid in the slums of New York," Reiss wrote. "And they wanted it the next day. I informed them huffily, 'A children's book is not a fast-food hamburger, and I am not McDonald's.'"

Then they offered to pay him $10,000. His response? "You want fries with that?"

While we can chuckle over the humor of his story, there's gold in it. Reiss demonstrates what some authors don't want to recognize: Sometimes we do what makes sense in the moment. Reiss didn't dream of writing *for* a celebrity; he dreamed of being a celebrity—at least in the minds of the kids who read his books and loved them. His passion didn't reside in pumping out a book in one day; it was in honing a great idea into a fun book with each word carefully chosen. And then rewriting until it was as good as he could make it.

But when an opportunity comes to make $10,000 in one day, well, pragmatism wins over passion. And that's not bad. Some authors who are stuck and can't get momentum going in their careers need to make a pragmatic move. That might be to write Harlequin romances for a season, letting sales numbers grow and learning from editors how to create a more compelling plotline. It might mean teaming with someone who has an inspiring message but not the ability to write it in a competent way.

One of my clients used to turn down opportunities to write as a collaborative author, but then money got tight—really tight—and she decided she would rather save her house than wait for a publisher to recognize her creative genius. She has kept busy and financially afloat ever since, and the last book she co-authored hit the best-seller list partly because of the name of the person she partnered with but also because my client wrote a beautiful book. And she carves out time in her busy schedule to work on a novel that's all hers that she's passionate about. Imagine how much stronger the possibilities are that I'll find a good home for it now that I can say she's recently written a best-selling book.

Making the pragmatic decision doesn't mean giving up on the dream; it does mean being willing to pursue that dream in ways you might not have anticipated. Setting aside your labor of love and establishing your name in other ways may be the most direct route to fulfilling your dreams.

PART EIGHT

The Inside Scoop on Marketing Strategies That Will Sell Copies of Your Book

CHAPTER 66

Hub Marketing and Why It Works

By Janet Kobobel Grant

Figuring out how to market effectively is one of the biggest challenges for writers. That's where hub marketing comes in.

When you set out to market something, **the first step is to establish your goal(s).**

For those of you who blew right past this point as being so obvious that it's eye-rolling worthy, pause a minute. It's surprising how seldom this step is actually taken. Stop and *really* decide what you want to achieve with your marketing.

The following are most likely answers for writers:

- Make people aware of my most recent release. Note: "Sell your most recent release" is your goal only if you're wanting to sell copies through your website and other venues. Most traditionally-published authors have little power to actually sell copies; that's what the publisher does.
- Build my blog readership. Or Increase blog readers' engagement. Or Increase blog subscriptions.
- Increase e-newsletter subscribers.
- Gain friends/followers/likes on a specific social medium.

Many of these goals are aimed at accomplishing something bigger that's outside your control, such as increasing book sales, obtaining an agent, or getting a publishing contract. Be sure to set goals *you* can attain.

Next, **employ hub marketing** to create your marketing plan. I call this marketing concept *hub marketing* because it creates a picture in your mind of how to organize your marketing campaign. Think in terms of a wheel (a Conestoga's or a Jaguar's or a Harley's—whatever appeals to you). The hub of the wheel is your goal. The spokes are the various marketing efforts that lead to your goal.

So, as the diagram below shows, if your goal is to build blog readership, you must drive people to your blog from other social media, using a variety of techniques.

By thinking in terms of hub marketing, you focus on your goal and how to pull every marketing possibility into the wheel as a spoke. This keeps you from thinking of Facebook, Twitter, YouTube, and even your home page as separate entities, some of which you "get" and others that mystify and defy you. Instead, they all are viewed as part of the wheel, and you become directed in how you're engaging in each one.

If you can't figure out how to use a particular wheel spoke to achieve your desired result, go back to that medium and see how someone else is using it to achieve what you have in mind. Or use a search engine to lead you to blogs that spell out, step-by-step, how to turn a social medium into a wheel spoke.

So set your goal and then create the wheel spokes that will funnel actions into the hub. Creating a marketing plan doesn't have to be complex if you think of it this way.

CHAPTER 67

The Author's and Publisher's Marketing Responsibilities

By Janet Kobobel Grant

Once a client of mine lamented that her publisher expected her to do all the heavy lifting when it came to publicizing her upcoming release. That conversation made me realize, once again, that authors have not grasped how publishers view each party's role in announcing a new book.

The Publisher's Job

The publisher sees its assignment as working the discoverability side of the equation. In other words, the publisher seeks ways to help readers discover you and your new book. This often is done in ways inaccessible to authors:

- Develop shelf talkers and offer them to bookstores (these are the little cards that appear below titles on a bookshelf, drawing attention to the book).
- Create a blog tour for you, utilizing the publisher's extensive list of influential bloggers.

- Bring book chain buyers to the publishing house to present new releases.
- Place Facebook or Goodreads ads targeting readers most likely to enjoy your book.
- Buy space for your book at the front of a bookstore such as certain Barnes & Noble. Endcaps, which are displays that appear generally at the ends of aisles, also are produced by the publisher and the space is "rented" for the endcap. (These efforts generally are reserved for titles expected to sell extremely well.)
- Buy a spot for your book in a book chain's newsletter or create a catalog of the publisher's newest titles to showcase them to library buyers.
- For those titles that are likely to be of particular interest to the media, hire an outside publicist who specializes in approaching significant talk shows about having you interviewed.
- Send books or ARCs (Advanced Reader Copies) to bloggers who attract the author's type of reader and ask for reviews (as well as submitting ARCs to significant publications such as *Publishers Weekly* and *Library Journal* for reviews).
- Offer copies of the book for the author to use in his or her publicity efforts. Often, the marketing team will provide bookmarks, flyers, and posters for the author, too. One of my clients, who wrote a book with a knitting theme, asked her publisher for and received hundreds of knitting needles with the book's title on them. (She had planned several publicity ideas using the needles.)

As you can see, the publisher concentrates efforts on widening your sphere of readers and providing you with the materials you need to do your own publicizing.

The Author's Job

The author is responsible for the care and feeding of his or her readers. In other words, once the publisher has convinced someone who has never read a book of yours to discover you, it becomes your job to make a personal connection with that reader. This is where you should concentrate your efforts.

- Welcome the readers to your website.
- Maintain those relationships through social media.
- Invite these readers to get to know you and open your world to them.
- Talk to them in your newsletter like they're your new best friends (because they are).

As an author, it is incredibly important to communicate with your audience. To give you a better sense of how to do that, Wendy has compiled a few suggestions.

CHAPTER 68

Gather Your Flock: Creating Your Reader List

By Wendy Lawton

As writers, we are creating something wonderful for our customers, for our readers. These are the most important people in our career universe. Not agents, not editors, not reviewers, not fellow writers—our audience is the reader. Our customer is the reader. I'll go one step further and say it's like a pastor and his congregation or a shepherd and his flock. Our readers are entrusted to us.

What data do we want to collect about them? In the best of all worlds, obtain your reader's name, physical address, phone number, email address, and website plus any data that will help you serve them. Normally you will only get a portion of this information.

You'll probably end up with more people on your e-list than on your physical mailing list. With the cost of postage, you might wonder, why collect physical addresses? For several reasons. If you are going to do a signing in a certain city, you can pull up all the zip codes in a certain-mile radius and send a postcard, telling of your event. Or, if you want to set a series in the geographic region where you have the biggest readership, you have that data at your fingertips. Maybe you need to do some research on street names in Poughkeepsie. Don't you think one of your readers would be delighted to be asked for help and then acknowledged in your book?

Pre-Published Author

From the time you first begin the journey toward becoming a published author, you need to be building your database of potential readers. How do you find readers if you've not yet written a book? If you write a blog, you have followers. If you speak at Rotary Clubs, you have listeners. If you teach a Sunday school class, you have those who come to hear you. They are all part of your flock. Make sure you don't fill your database only with other writers' names. Yes, you may want them there, but they are not your primary reader.

Published Author

From the time your book first comes out, you'll begin collecting names of readers. If they write you a letter, collect the info. If you spend time with a research librarian, add her to the list. When people send you emails, thank them and ask if you can keep their email address to let them know when your next book comes out. When you speak or do signings, have a two-part card designed. The top half has a picture of your book or books and a note promising you'll let them know when you are next in the area or when the next book comes out. You also want to reassure them on this top half that you will keep their information private, only using it to let them know what's happening in your world. The tear-off part is what they put in the hopper for a chance to win the amazing door prize you've brought. Or they hand it to your helper. It asks for all the information you'd love to have for your database.

Let's make a list of whom you'll add and how you might get their information:

Blog Readers	Create a giveaway to collect names/email addresses
Speaking Event Attendees	Have a sign-up sheet at the back of the room
Speaking Event Attendees	Door prize: Collect physical addresses and email

Speaker Event Attendees	Have a two-part postcard to pass out—one part for them, one part for you
Book Store Signings	Have a sign-up sheet on your table
Book Store Signings	Great door prize: Collect physical addresses and email
Book Store Signings	Have a two-part postcard to pass out—one for them, one for you
Facebook	Host an approved giveaway or promotion
Book Clubs	Bring a basket of friends' books as a door prize: Collect names
Reader Letters	Collect the return address, etc.
Website Visitors	Set up a guestbook that automatically collects the data

Once you have a list, here's how you will use it:

- **First off, you will never, ever share this database with anyone.** These people contacted you, and they deserve your care. They are your unique flock, not a flock for rent. You will not even share this list with your publisher any more than they would share their database with you. If you let your publisher have these names, they'd naturally add them to their master list, and your flock would soon run toward the hills, bleating piteously as they hear the confusing voices of hundreds of other potential shepherds.
- **Contact them by email, by mail—whatever works best.** These readers were interested enough to contact you, to participate in your giveaway, or to come to see you. They, at the very least, deserve to know when a book is coming out. Take care of this flock. Be personable. Share bits of your life with them. Be strategic. If your list is big enough and all these readers flock to the

store the first week your book is out, you will make the best-seller list.

- Remember, if you are going to be doing a signing in a certain city, pull up all the zip codes in a 200-mile radius and **send a colorful book postcard**, telling of your event and allowing them to use the postcard to get a free gift or enter the drawing twice or something equally special. That way you'll collect the postcards bearing the names of your uber-readers—the ones who will get in a car and drive to come see you. If you someday need to assemble a group of marketing mavens/meisters, these are the readers most likely to be on it.

And that's just a start.

CHAPTER 69

The Trouble with Promoting Your Author-Friends' Books

By Wendy Lawton

Someone recently contacted me with this marketing question:

I have a notion I struggle with, and can't quite figure how to think about...and that is authors cross-promoting. I debuted last year and have a four-book contract. Many authors (without my asking) promoted my book on Facebook, which I appreciated, but their audience is different than mine, and I didn't see a lot of web hits coming from those authors' Facebook posts. Now, I'm being asked to return the favor. As a good friend...I want to. BUT... at least one of my reader friends on FB privately mentioned she hates when there is TOO much book promoting going on, and she was glad I refrained from that. Sigh...what's an author to do? Frankly, my preference is just to let each author connect with their own tribe/audience so there's not so much noise. But, I don't want to risk alienating peer authors.

Good question. How much cross-promoting should an author do? Let me start by repeating what I wrote in the previous chapter:

- **Never, never, never share your reader list with anyone.** This is your most valuable asset as a writer. You will work hard to gather each name and to keep this list fresh. You will faithfully input every reader name, email address, and physical address in your database. The important thing to remember is this is your list. You've made an unspoken (or maybe even written) promise to these people that you won't share their names with anyone. Never plan a cross-promotion during which you give another writer—or even your publisher—these names.
- Decide how many times you can cross-promote without its costing you. In other words, if each day you feature another friend's book, pretty soon you are going to wear people out. When your book releases, it will look like just one of 365 other books you talk about.
- When you decide what number of other authors you can cross-promote, make sure that a) you are crazy about them and their writing, b) they share a similar audience with you, and c) the promotion you do for their books sounds genuine and heartfelt—like a friend recommending a book to friends.
- Make sure the handful of authors who will be your cross-promotional partners also present your books in a genuine, winsome way.
- When other authors ask you to promote their books, just tell them that you can only handle a limited number of cross-promotional partners, but since you love their books (if you do) you'll put them on a list. If one of your current partners goes off to a new genre or stops writing, you have a list of possible new partners. And, in the process, you've not hurt anyone's feelings.
- Of course, if your publisher comes up with a cross-promotional event, you gladly take part. Many marketing departments are coming up with fun contests and events that pull together a

number of their authors—this would be a different strategy than blogging about individual authors' books.

It's difficult to strike the balance between helping others and keeping the promotional noise at a comfortable level, but not saying yes to every opportunity and not saying no to every opportunity is a way to begin to find that balance for you.

CHAPTER 70

Tapping into the Power of Word of Mouth

By Janet Kobobel Grant

Studies consistently show that word of mouth—one person advocating to another to try a product—is the most powerful marketing tool that exists. We employ others' recommendations to select books, movies, and TV programs. But more than that, we actually *ask* for suggestions. "Please market to me," we in essence are saying.

We all have go-to people in our lives—the folks who have the same reading and/or viewing tastes as we do. For example, when I'm at a loss as to what to read next, I ask one of my co-workers. She's a prolific reader, and while she and I don't always agree on how much we like a book, she has stimulating suggestions.

It's all well and good to know that word of mouth is powerful, but how do you, as an author, tap into it consistently and effectively?

- **Deliver the goods.** If you write a strong manuscript time after time, you develop a following. And those who discover your books want to show how smart and insightful they are by telling their friends about you. They are choosing to attach their reading reputation to your writing reputation, which is exactly what you want.

- **Connect rather than collect.** Avoid the trap of working to collect "likes," whatever form they may take. That's just a statistic. Instead, concentrate on how to connect with your readers. In a *Forbes* article on the power of word of mouth, Suzanne Fanning, President of Word of Mouth Marketing Association, advises, "Give your fans the gift of you." That sums up how to approach each opportunity to connect with your readers, whether that's online or in person.

I remember an author telling me about a book signing she had in which only a handful of readers turned out. Despite the small number, she describes it as the best book signing she's ever had because she had the opportunity to connect on a deeper level with each person. I just know those fans increased their loyalty and enthusiasm multiple times because of that event.

- **Give them reasons to talk.** Be funny, be inspirational, be open. Don't be afraid to let readers get to know the real you. Above all, provide them with material they can talk about, whether online or in person. "It really depends on you understanding your consumers and what they like about you and providing whatever it is they need from you," Fanning observes.

I appreciate that she specifies the importance of knowing: a) what readers like about you and b) what they need from you. Those are two different elements and can help you to decide what you share about yourself.

And it helps to direct *how* you write and *what* you write about.

I remember a few years ago walking with a friend several blocks in San Francisco to a restaurant. A man was shoving his way through the crowds of people, and it occurred to me that, if he happened onto someone with physical challenges, the man might well ruthlessly push that person aside.

"You should put that guy in one of your novels and make him infamous," I joked to her.

She responded, "Oh, no, I'd never put someone so nasty in one of my books. My readers don't like that sort of person."

I was surprised at the adamant way my friend was taking care of her readers. But I appreciated that she would never foist a character on them they had no interest in meeting. She knows what her readers like about her (she's seriously nice) and what they need from her (uplifting stories).

- **Give readers a voice.** Ask them to vote for their favorite cover design, to name a character, to choose a title. Use your imagination as to ways to invite readers to invest in the creative process with you.

Fanning points out in the *Forbes* article: "Lay's is an excellent example to highlight how they empowered their fans to 'Do Us a Flavor,' and allow consumers to create a new flavor of potato chips to hit store shelves. Over 3.8 million submissions were sent in 2013, making it one of the biggest marketing campaigns for PepsiCo-owned Frito-Lay."

- **Promote others.** Help others to be successful, especially those who garner the same sort of reader you do. Yes, we're talking about your competitors. By building them up, you're establishing yourself as an influencer, a voice to pay attention to. And when you help others, they, in turn, will want to help you. Not to mention that it's a gracious way to behave. (See Wendy's previous chapter on promoting author-friends' books for further details.)
- **Ask readers to show off how much they love your book(s).** Put together a Facebook or Instagram photo contest with readers in various settings holding your book. You could create several categories of winners so more than one person could earn a prize. Ask your readers to then share with their friends and followers a video you provide on how your cover was made. Becky Wade created "How This Cover Was Made" videos for each of her recent releases. Whenever I see that she has a new book out, I trot over to her website to watch the video.

Use your creativity to figure out how to start word-of-mouth promotion of your book. Be true to who you are as an author and also to what your readers want from you.

CHAPTER 71

How Important Is a Writer's Social Media Presence?

By Janet Kobobel Grant

Publishers care about your social media presence. They care a lot. Actually, they probably care too much. Here's why: **The majority of them don't know how to judge if your presence will actually result in book sales.**

Let's say, for example, you have 50,000 likes on Facebook. A publisher might consider that number decent. If you have 100,000 likes, that might move the dial into the respectable zone, and the publisher would be more prone to want to offer you a contract.

During a recent meeting I had with an editor, she mentioned that she had to see a strong number of social media connections before she could take a writer's project to the publishing committee.

"What would be considered strong?" I asked.

"A million," the editor said nonchalantly. As if that number were common, ordinary.

What!? Really!?

What drove me crazy was this: **The editor wasn't looking for a meaningful number, just for a magic one.** One that would result in her being able to offer a contract.

Let's be blunt. **Numbers can be bought.** I located a site recently where, for $5, a person with hundreds of thousands of Twitter followers will do a tweet about you. Presumably you could hire the person to tweet a link to your blog. Or he could tweet suggesting his followers follow you.

Will traffic increase to your blog by buying clicks? Will you gain hundreds of thousands of new followers? Would those numbers have any meaning? Facebook likes don't translate into book sales. Kissmetrics pooled data from a variety of sources to show that business and fan page likes are relatively meaningless when it comes to generating revenue.

A smart publisher looks beneath the surface and wants numbers that have meaning. How can you generate meaningful numbers?

- **Work to create actual engagement on social media.** This could be the number of shares from a Facebook post or number of comments to a Facebook post or clicks on links offered on a variety of social media. Showing that conversations and real connections are occurring can make a smaller number more meaningful than a large number that doesn't indicate engagement.
- **Pay attention to the percentage of books sold at author events.** If, when you speak in person, your ratio of number of books sold to number of attendees is high, that's a meaningful number.
- **Build the size of your newsletter list.** When a reader signs up for your newsletter, that's a commitment considerably bigger than liking you on Facebook. The newsletter will pop up in that person's email. Who among us is longing to increase the amount of email we receive? We ask for newsletters only from those we really want to hear from. You can also report the open rate for your newsletters.
- **Show actual increase in book sales from a marketing effort.** If you appear on a radio program and your book's Amazon ranking shifts from #198,348 to #5,309 in the ensuing hours, the likelihood that the interview had an effect is pretty high.

- **Report on webinar attendees.** If you offer a webinar, especially one for which attendees need to pay, the number who sign up is an indication of whether you are viewed as a spokesperson—on the topic of your book, of course; otherwise the webinar number isn't nearly as meaningful.
- **Communicate that your numbers are trending upward.** If you're building blog readers steadily over a year, that suggests you're gaining traction and creating connections with potential buyers of your book.

Whenever possible, I talk to acquisitions editors and publishing executives about how numbers are not all created equally. The easy decision is to look at readily attainable numbers such as likes and followers. But who said easy is smart?

As a final bit of advice on social media numbers, John Moore, marketer for Starbucks and Whole Foods says, "If people are not talking about you, they are forgetting about you."

But sometimes being consumed with online engagement can backfire, as Wendy demonstrates in the next chapter.

CHAPTER 72

Marketing Gone Wrong: The Balance Between Marketing and Writing

By Wendy Lawton

A few years back a frustrated editor commented to me about a writer we knew. The warning bears repeating. The editor said, "I just wish he would spend less time networking—tweeting and Facebooking— and more time writing a book that takes it to the next level."

Eek! We are always telling our authors to build a significant presence on the social networks. A platform. We want you to Facebook, to tweet, to blog and to keep up your website. It's part of building community, right? And community is potential readership. I mean, we've all read Seth Godin's *Tribes,* and if we haven't jumped into the blogosphere, we feel guilty about our electronic slothfulness.

What does one do with a comment like the editor's though?

There's an unspoken story here. It has more to do with the quality of the book being turned in than the online marketing the author is doing. This particular author is very visible on every writing blog and every social network.

This editor actually loves connected writers, but she was pointing out a dangerous imbalance. I call it playing around the edges. There are too many writers who love the cachet of being an author; they just don't like the work of writing. They'd much rather talk with other writers, sip exotic coffees in literary coffee houses, and just play around the edges of writing. It's a dangerous business if you hope to build a career.

How can you tell if you are a diligent networker (which is important for a successful career) or just playing around the edges (which can be a career killer)?

You might be playing around the edges if:

- You like doing Facebook, Twitter, Pinterest, and blogs far better than writing your manuscript.
- You are spending more time online talking about writing to other writers than connecting with your readers.
- Your blog is all about writing instead of about topics of interest to your readers. (Your readers are more interested in the things you write about and in you than they are in how you write.)
- You can blow off an impending deadline to have lunch with a fellow writer or go to a conference.

See the pattern? If writing comes first, you have no worries. If you love the writing community or the online community far more than the solitary work of writing, you may have some soul searching to do. No matter how much we talk about connecting, it's the writing that will ultimately insure success or be a career killer.

CHAPTER 73

Marketing Gone Wrong: A Marketing Flop and What to Learn from It

By Janet Kobobel Grant

I remember when Wendy outed on Facebook the first car I owned when I was a high school student. Unlike Wendy's first car, a perky '57 MGA convertible, I drove…an Edsel.

Yes, the car with such a bad reputation that, when you look it up in the dictionary, one of its definitions is "a poor or unsuccessful product, especially if vigorously promoted." In my defense, the vehicle was our family's car until my father purchased a new one, and he dumped the embarrassing Edsel on me. I wondered if I could drive into the school parking lot in the dark of night, sleep in the boat-sized car, and then drift into the school building early enough for my classmates not to connect me with the Edsel.

For those who don't know the car's history, here's a primer.

The Ford Motor Company created the Edsel amid a muscular marketing campaign, proclaiming it to be an "entirely new kind of car." The day it was presented to the public, "E Day," on September 4, 1957, the windows of the dealerships were papered shut. The only way to view the car was to stand in a line that snaked around the block, with a few people admitted at a time. After a massive campaign that included multi-page "teaser" ads in major national magazines, 2.5 million Americans poured into Edsel dealerships.

Much to everyone's surprise the car looked...average. Like any other car. Except for the silly, horse-collar-shaped front grill.

The car truly was innovative, offering design features never seen before, and some we've come to expect in our vehicles today. The massive list included:

- a rolling-dome speedometer
- warning lights for such conditions as low oil level, parking brake engaged, and engine overheating
- push-button Teletouch transmission shifting system in the center of the steering wheel
- ergonomically designed controls for the driver
- self-adjusting brakes
- safety features such as seat belts and child-proof rear door locks that could only be opened with the key

But the public had come to expect something never seen before, startling and beyond imagining. A pancake-flipping, make-your-bed-in-the-morning, and drive itself sort of car. The Edsel couldn't live up to the hype. It was, as a matter of fact, short-lived, from 1957 to1960.

What can we learn from the Edsel boondoggle?

One of the most stunning aspects of the Edsel story is that **Ford had no idea the car's sales would be lackluster**. Instead, they were anticipating a booming success. Executives did research on what the public wanted when they started to design the car, but I've found no evidence they asked for feedback during the process. Instead, they seem to have made decisions based on what their gut said was right.

For example, they did extensive polling on a **name for the car**, but when it came down to the final choice, the results were inconclusive so an executive went with "Edsel." The name of Henry Ford's son, *Edsel* is a clunky word, not one that causes the potential purchaser to think about a smooth-riding, debonair car to coast around town in. Even Henry Ford II objected to its use. By the way, some of the other names under consideration were Citation, Corsair, Pacer, and Ranger.

Lesson: Consider what a title or name tells a potential buyer to expect from your book. Make sure the title projects the right image. Survey potential readers and then pay attention to what they tell you. Don't make decisions in a closet and pop out of it with manuscript in hand, never having ascertained if you were assembling the most attractive book possible.

Ford also misjudged **what the public would pay for the car.** The extra features cost so much that interested buyers, on hearing the price, turned around and walked out of the dealerships in search of a more affordable automobile. Ford hadn't asked consumers what they would pay for a car with the Edsel's features.

Lesson: We all know consumers are price sensitive. While the market will bear high prices for significant innovation, the question always is this: Will the consumer think he will get his money's worth with my product? Asking would be a good way to find out.

The Edsel came off the production lines at a time when consumers were thinking about smaller, fuel-efficient cars; in fact, the Volkswagen Beetle was gaining in popularity. The Edsel, on the other hand, was a much larger car, required premium gasoline, and was fuel-inefficient: It was **the right car at the wrong time.**

Lesson: This one is tricky because, when Ford started to develop the Edsel in 1955, its size and other characteristics were what customers wanted. But it took until 1957 to release the first models. Tastes had changed, and a recession had hit. Perhaps the best lesson we can gain is to assume that a product will need to be adjusted if it takes a long time to produce. Keeping up with changing tastes and being flexible are paramount, especially in our rapidly changing world.

Design oddities also created challenges for the Edsel. The push button transmission confused drivers because it was located where they used to find the car's horn. The driver who meant to tap his horn could actually put the car in reverse. The station wagon's rear turn signals were boomerang-shaped and, when seen from a distance, gave the impression the car was turning right rather than left and vice versa. And then people had a lot of fun coming up with ways to describe the odd-shaped front grill design, including a toilet seat and the "O" of an Oldsmobile sucking a lemon.

Lesson: Always remember that while it's one thing to be innovative, it's another to be odd. Doing something different for the sake of being different seldom results in something good.

The hype, of course, has to be mentioned as a major fail. Huge amounts of marketing dollars went into a campaign based almost exclusively on promising the extraordinary and on setting up a teaser campaign.

Lesson: I'm personally weary of the hype promos we see online: Webinar ads promising that, if we attend, we'll learn the 5 Vital Ways to Kickstart Our Social Media; the Must-Know Secrets to Writing a Best-seller, etc. Stop the hype and make promises you can fulfill.

After examining the reasons the Edsel failed, I think it's only fair to say that our family owned a 1959 model, which adjusted many of the first year's oddities. It was a great car to drive, and mine happened to be a pretty turquoise. I kind of liked it, just as I would have liked an odd but interesting cousin. I would have been further consoled if my father had let me sell the car that had become a collector's dream when I purchased my spunky red 1964 Ford Mustang. But, no, he had decided to give the Edsel to his sister, who was a car collector. Insult to injury.

CHAPTER 74

Marketing Gone Wrong: When Marketing Goes Too Far

By Janet Kobobel Grant

I recently saw two marketing ideas that generated a lot of online noise. They did so because they crossed an invisible line—the line that causes potential customers to be repelled.

Both marketing ploys were contests.

The first one drew such negative publicity that the contest was canceled. Publisher Hachette's Australian division ran a "tatvertising" campaign for the release of Stieg Larsson's book, *The Girl in the Spider Web*. The plan was to select an individual who would have a large image of a dragon tattooed to cover his or her entire back. The "tat" would be used in the advertising campaign.

However, when media and individuals panned the idea, the publisher decided people were viewing the campaign as tacky or even worse—as taking advantage of the winner. So the tattoo portion of the campaign disappeared, even though the publisher stated the contest had generated a lot of interest from potential tattoo-ees.

The second negative marketing idea was a baby-naming contest. BJ's Restaurant and Brewhouse, which has 169 restaurants around the country, offered one lucky couple a $10,000 gift certificate to BJ's if they were the first to name their baby Quinoa. "We are so excited to introduce these amazing new Quinoa Bowls that we wanted to do something big, maybe even a little crazy," Chief Marketing Officer Kevin Maye said in a statement.

Yeah, "crazy" would be the operative word. The contest's rules specified that Quinoa had to be the child's first name and that a birth certificate had to be shown before the gift certificate was bestowed. And if you weren't the first to do so, well, you've just done your child no favors, as that cute little one would move through life as *Quinoa* with no special privileges at BJ's.

In my online search for articles about the Quinoa contest, I found some favorable to the idea, some neutral, and others unhesitatingly against.

These two instances are extreme examples of marketing. They beg the questions: What makes marketing effective? What pushes it over the top?

To counterbalance those marketing kerfuffles, in the last month, two of my clients were each asked by their publisher to participate in a specific marketing idea. Both clients said no. One was being asked to have a booth at an event where many potential readers of her book would attend. That was outside her comfort zone, and she was afraid to try something new. The other was asked to step outside his convenience zone—the time of the event required him to rise really early, but he would be meeting buyers from a significant bookstore chain.

Both decisions had a chilling effect on the marketing/publicity team. It's hard work to find significant marketing opportunities. Hearing "No thanks" rather than "Thank you!" tends to discourage marketing folks.

Authors regularly face the question, "Is this important enough for me to do regardless of my hesitancy?" But it's a question few actually take the time to ask themselves.

It would make sense to ask:

- Is this marketing/publicity idea one my readers would be enthusiastic about?
- Might it have a down side (e.g., tatvertising)?

- Does it draw attention to my book, or is it so exotic that my book is overshadowed?
- Even if it's a new venture for me, does it make sense to do it rather than cool marketing's enthusiasm?
- Is my inconvenience in participating in this marketing idea minor compared to the potential outcome?

PART NINE

At Long Last! The Inside Scoop on Your Book Launch

CHAPTER 75

Celebrate! The Uber-Creative Book Launch

By Wendy Lawton

I recently read an article about a business that does nothing but help engineer out-of-the-box marriage proposals. Apparently there is more pressure than ever to create a never-to-be-forgotten event in which to pop the question. In the article, Vanessa Kiely of WeddingIndustryExperts.com said, "With the spread of social media, people feel not only pressured to take their proposals to a new level but excited by the possibilities of doing something truly original. They want a story they can share for years to come."

It made me think about engineering fabulous book launches. A story to share for years to come.

Several Books & Such clients have recently had wonderful book launches. They've pulled out all the stops to make the day special. Forget popping the question. Nothing is more worthy of celebrating these days than having a book published. And if it is your debut book, put on a show-stopper. Let's look at several benefits for planning an uber-creative book launch event:

- A book launch is the perfect way to not only have the fun of the event but also to thank all those who've journeyed with you.

- You'll be able to leverage the event by talking about it on social media, posting pictures, and connecting in social media to those who attended. It's nonthreatening publicity for your book.
- Because you'll have some sort of drawing or registration, you'll be collecting interested readers for your database.
- Another reason to have a unique launch is to potentially interest the media. It's hard to get your newspaper or television station to come to an event, but you can often get the echo effect of media coverage afterward by providing a great press release and photos: "Local Author Holds Standing Room Only Event."
- Some authors have worked a philanthropic angle into their launch, which always interests the media.
- Others do something so unique that the media just have to cover it.

So who plans the event, the publisher or the author? Let's look at a typical question an agent might hear: "I don't get it. My friend's publisher put together a wildly creative event for the launch of her new crime novel. It was held at a big city police station with donuts and coffee for all plus free books and a generous donation to the Police Athletics League. All her friends came. The police officers loved it. Even the homeless came and enjoyed the donuts. Why won't my publisher organize some of the innovative events I want?"

It's all a matter of perspective. Every book has a set marketing budget. As an agent I cringe when the author talks the publisher into doing an "innovative event" that uses a hefty portion of the budget for what could be considered a vanity event. Take the above (fictitious) event. It would draw friends, who would have purchased the book anyway unless their friend, the author, gifted them with it. The event also would have honored the police, and a few of them might be readers, but if most of the officers are men, the odds are not great that they'd become a fan of a romance. The homeless might have read the book given them but would not have been in the position of influencing others. The only way that event could justify the investment would be if local news coverage reached more potential readers than typical marketing would have. Many of the innovative things we cook up can't hold a candle to, say, sending ARCs (advance reading copies) to reviewers, librarians, and influencers.

So, if the uber-creative launch is up to you, what out-of-the-box idea will garner attention and actually accomplish the benefits I listed above?

- **Take a clue from your book.** My client, Sarah Loudin Thomas, announced the release of her first Appalachian novel, *Miracle in a Dry Season*, with the perfect launch. The book is about a woman, Perla, who settles in a 1950s poor, hungry community. Perla convinces people to bring what they have to the general store to share with everyone. She's a marvelous cook, but something miraculous seems to happen each time she cooks. There's more than enough food for everyone to eat their fill with leftovers to take home. This eventually gets her in trouble, of course.

  Because the author works at a nonprofit home for children, she charged for the event and invited people from the community and her nonprofit as well as friends and family. What did she serve? Southern beans and cornbread, much like her character might have served. Because she was making money for the nonprofit, the media covered it, and her book received a very nice launch.
- **Pick a venue that will draw.** Another client, Tessa Afshar, held her event for *Harvest of Gold* at the Mark Twain House and Museum in Connecticut. She could have filled the lecture hall by herself with local fans, but the museum also featured the event and publicized it to their members and visitors. She had an elegant launch with an overflow crowd and sold cartons of books.
- **Pull off an over-the-top stunt.** Debbie Macomber introduced her Christmas novella one year in a mega bookstore by having

a conga line of twenty-five Santas. It was not something soon forgotten.

- **Involve those in attendance**. Sarah Sundin celebrated the launch of her World War II novel, *Through Waters Deep*, at a Barnes & Noble store. She gave a book talk and had refreshments, but as soon as the talk was over, employees came and cleared away the chairs and Sarah's Books & Such literary agent, Rachel Kent, who taught swing dance in her college years, and her dance partner taught several dances to those in attendance. The crowds couldn't help but gather as "Boogie Woogie Bugle Boy" played throughout the store and the sidewalk beyond. Readers loved it.

The possibilities are only limited by the limits of your imagination and budget. But it's an unforgettable way to celebrate this important milestone, and when you draw on friends and readers to help you pull it off, you give them ownership in the success of your book. Be creative!

CHAPTER 76

Using a Book Launch Team

By Janet Kobobel Grant

Seth Godin talks about building a tribe; Michael Hyatt talks about creating a launch team. Both concepts contain the same nugget of truth: If you want to drive sales, you need a crowd of influencers to spread the word. But do these concepts really work for book launches?

I interviewed two of my clients who each created a launch team for a book release: DiAnn Mills, who released a suspense, *The Survivor*, and Tricia Goyer, with two new releases, *The Promise Box* (a novel) and *Lead Your Family Like Jesus* (a nonfiction book coauthored with Ken Blanchard and Phil Hodges).

Both Tricia and DiAnn started out with a big plus: They have developed tribes through their social media venues.

Here are their responses to the questions I thought you would have:

How did you form your launch team?

Tricia: I first heard about launch teams on Michael Hyatt's blog. I used Survey Monkey to ask four questions. I contacted bloggers I know to take the survey, tweeted about the survey and mentioned it on Facebook. I formed two teams: one for fiction and one for nonfiction. I have several books releasing this year so I asked each person to participate for a year. Anyone who wanted to be on the team needed to fill out the survey saying what they could do to help to launch a book. 170 people applied; I picked 100.

Hyatt suggested making the team exclusive, hard to get into. But, looking back, I found probably half participated; a quarter of the team was really involved. Now I'd take everyone on because I realize not everyone will stay interested.

DiAnn: I began with a letter circulated through my e-newsletter, Twitter, and Facebook. Ninety-eight people are on my team. They're fans, book reviewers, bloggers, bookstore owners, and book club leaders. I'd hoped for a dozen. Although I was concerned with such a large group, it's worked well. I've closed the group at this number but recognize that, as time goes on, some will choose to drop their participation.

How do you communicate with your group and what do you ask them to do?

DiAnn: We're a Yahoo group. My team has arranged book club events, speaking engagements, attended book signings, written reviews, and promoted my books and me via social media.

Tricia: We have a private FB group for coordination. I post a schedule for each release with a to-do list for them each day. There are days they post questions on their blogs about the book with my answers. On other days they post reviews. At first I asked for promo ideas but found people generally just want to be directed.

What incentives do you give people who join your team?

DiAnn: Each week I provide the team with an inspirational essay I've written. We also do book club discussions. I've invited team members to submit their own essay to me, and I'll edit them and share them with the group. I also have contests just for them and announce upcoming events to them before anyone else. They, of course, get advance copies of my books to review.

Tricia: Each person gets a free copy of the book ahead of time. They really like that. If someone goes above and beyond what I've asked, that person gets a surprise gift—a gift certificate to shop at an online site or a Starbucks gift certificate, and I'll announce to the group who won a prize and why.

I've also found that people like to interact with the author. Just responding to their comments on our Facebook page keeps them engaged.

Would you use a launch team again?

Tricia: Yes! Lots of people are getting the word out about your book for you. They were creative, like coming up with quotes from *Lead Your Family Like Jesus* for Pinterest and for tweeting. I probably would have overlooked those quotes, but the team's fresh eyes saw them. One woman on the *Lead Like Jesus* team asked her blog readers to take a 14-day challenge to pray in specific ways for their children and then report back. It's exciting for me to be part of the team too.

DiAnn: Absolutely! It's all about relationships, and we've bonded into a wonderful, supportive group in which we celebrate birthdays and care about what happens in each other's lives.

THE FINAL SCOOP:

The Good News!

By Wendy Lawton

If you've stayed with us for this whole book, you might be reeling at this point. You may be ready to cross "write a book" off your bucket list. Who knew you would have to be a marketer, an industry observer, and a social media guru, all while still keeping your day job? And nobody told you it would be so hard to get an agent or sell a manuscript, right?

I want to close by telling you that the news is not all bad.

Good News: Pent-up Publisher Buying Demand

We are going to reap the results of a pent-up buying demand on the part of publishers. They have been very conservative, very risk-averse for quite some time. A couple of years ago, some publishers cut how many titles they released each season, causing an overstock of contracted books. All of that—cutting and overstock—is drawing to a close.

When I was in the toy industry, one retailer used to say, "You can't sell from an empty shelf" each time she placed her hefty order. Wise words. Every business needs to have great product. Janet and I have sat in a number of different meetings when publishing representatives have offered variations of, "We're going to publish fewer books but put more behind the books we do publish. Fewer books but bigger sales for those books."

Yeah, right.

When we hear that, it takes everything we've got not to snicker—as if a publisher could predict which books would break out and only publish those potentially big books. We all pride ourselves on our gut instincts, but the only way to really identify a best-seller is to get the book out there and see what it does. If my retailer friend were to advise publishers she would say, "You can't sell from an empty catalog."

So How Is That Good News?

We're seeing an uptick in book sales to publishing houses. They are buying. If you are a writer with books to sell, this is a good thing. We're expecting to see publishers begin to add to their catalogs. The only way to discover more best-sellers is to develop a broader offering. The more gallons of milk in the tank, the more cream that will rise to the top, right?

But that's not the end of my good news. The demise of the publishing industry has been greatly exaggerated. And I think the chances of your becoming a published author have never been better.

Don't Wish for the Good Old Days

During the last century, to be published, an author would have to type his manuscript with a carbon copy, or in the pre-carbon copy days re-type his whole manuscript, and deliver the manuscript to one mysterious editor at a time. And wait. You've heard the term "over the transom" submissions referring to unsolicited manuscripts, but in those days, the bundled manuscript was sometimes literally launched over an open transom into the cramped editorial office of a publisher.

Business etiquette was of a more genteel nature so most likely the hopeful author would have received a personal, hand-typed reply. Washington Irving received the following rejection letter when he asked a long-silent editor if he could have his materials back.

My Dear Sir,

I entreat you to believe that I feel truly obliged by your kind intentions toward me, and that I entertain the most unfeigned respect for your most tasteful talents. My house is completely filled with work people at this time, and I have only an office to transact business in; and yesterday I was wholly occupied, or I should have done myself the pleasure of seeing you.

If it would not suit me to engage in the publication of your present work it is only because I do not see that scope in the nature of it which would enable me to make those satisfactory accounts between us, without which I really feel no satisfaction in engaging—but I will do all I can to promote their circulation, and shall be most ready to attend to any future plan of yours.

With much regard, I remain, dear sir,
Your faithful servant,
John Murray

Translation: *Sorry it has taken me so long to get back to you. I've been swamped. No matter how I crunch the numbers, the bottom line on the pro forma doesn't work for our house.*

Much has changed over the years. Although, looking at the letter above, much has stayed the same. But let's talk about the changes. . .

Since the advent of the home computer, manuscripts can be sent with one keystroke to legions of agents or editors at one time. For those of us on the receiving end, this has exponentially increased our submissions to the point of not even being able to personally respond. They say the age of gentility ended in 1910, but in publishing, it ended with the age of the home computer.

But Here's the Good News

The computer ushered in a world where the agent or editor is no longer an ominous figure locked away in a shabby, walnut-paneled office somewhere in Manhattan or London. The publishing world is now transparent via the Internet. Publishers, editors, and agents are blogging daily, revealing all—insider secrets, systems, workarounds, and preferences. It's all there for the taking! Can you imagine the choices Washington Irving could have made with information like that?

And There's More Good News

With social media, finding an agent is no longer a one-way street. We are constantly connecting and observing writers online. A while ago I commented to Janet that I was impressed by everything written in the comments section of our blog by a certain writer. I told her I was thinking of contacting the writer because if her book was half as good as her ability to connect, she'd be a great success. Janet just laughed. One of my colleagues at Books & Such had already snatched this writer up.

I can't imagine anything like that happening a century ago unless you met an agent or an editor in person at a soiree, a salon, or a dinner party. It's an exciting new world filled with opportunities to connect in fresh ways.

Even More Good News

A century ago, people didn't travel as we do today. Writers, agents, and editors gather together in person more than ever before. Forget the dinner party: You can now spend an entire week with your favorite publishing professionals, practice the craft, and learn about the business of writing. Agents and editors are committed to making ourselves available at writers conferences. It's my favorite way to meet writers who are willing to invest time, energy, and fiscal resources in their careers.

The Good News Rolls On: Someone Left the Gate Open

Writers used to rail against the gatekeepers in publishing. And gatekeepers are legion. You've heard the complaints from writers: "You can't get to the publishers without an agent, and you can't get an agent without being published." (For the record, neither of these is true.) I've also heard publishers moan about the bookstore buyers as gatekeepers. If a powerful chain doesn't like a cover, the book is dead in the water. Or if a conservative bookstore owner takes exception to content, the publisher will never be able to sell that author into that store again. Gatekeepers!

With so many new ways to publish, the gates have been flung wide open. If you can't get an agent or a publisher to take notice, you can self-publish and distribute your own book. Or, you can self-publish as an e-book. Or you can do a combination of the two and make your book available as a POD (print-on-demand) physical book and an e-book. Or a self-published physical edition and an e-book.

Voilà! Gatekeepers banished. With no one standing in your way, you are completely responsible for your own success. It's a big responsibility since you are accountable for brilliant writing, a gorgeous cover, perfect editing, and dazzling marketing. But the upside is that no one will slam a gate in your face.

We're not Done with Good News

With an investment commitment, some of the above can be outsourced. It's a far different world than the shuttered halls of yesterday's publishing. You don't need to have an agent or a publisher for you to hold your book in your hands or to download to your e-reader. You are free to fly.

So, Do We Agents Worry That We Will Become Obsolete?

Not at all. Our work is value added to the writer. There is a substantial return on every penny of commission I receive. We may be considered gatekeepers by some, but to our clients we are more like a doorman—we open doors for them. We also help to brainstorm, coach, plan careers, encourage, run interference, collect money, negotiate contracts, and make important decisions. And as the industry changes, our unique contributions remain valuable. We are constantly evolving—creating innovative tools for our clients and developing all new strategies for success. Who knows what literary agenting will look like over the next few years? It's exciting!

It is the same with publishers. Once a writer begins publishing on his own, he will come to value the many things publishers now do on his behalf even more. Who wants to spend time securing ISBN numbers and writing press releases? Yes, writers can do it all, but will a writer do it all and still write? That's one of the nagging questions that remains to be seen.

So while questions remain, possibilities seem limitless for writers ready to take their seed of an idea and create a finished manuscript that finds its way into the hands of readers through traveling the traditional publishing paths or through newly trodden ones.

It's an exciting new world out there. Good news, indeed.

Acknowledgments

Since agents don't sit around tapping their fingers on their desks, wondering how to entertain themselves next, the only way we could have created this book was by teaming up with talented people in a collaborative effort. Among those who made this book possible are:

Olivia Butze, who stepped into the role of pulling our varied and scattered thoughts on publishing into a real book, with a flow that made sense.

David Butze, who encouraged us to pursue offering publication helps through a book and kindly kept us on course.

Kimberly Drake and Vicki Klopsch at Scripps College, a member of the Claremont Colleges, who supported the idea of our teaching a "Writing as Business" multi-day seminar, and managed the many details to make it happen and to promote it to the students. The students who attended our seminar and helped us to decide what was valuable and what was expendable; thanks for your eagerness to listen and to learn.

Janet McHenry, who edited the manuscript with care and competency.

The team at FaceOut Studio, who were a dream team of creative, intelligent, and fun book cover designers. And The DESK's Katherine Lloyd, who quickly, competently, and creatively designed *The Inside Scoop's* interior. You made us look good!

Ginny Smith, for walking us through the details of publishing this book despite our ongoing delays. Without your help, we would be stalled at square one.

Our clients, who keep us on our toes and thinking creatively about how to make them successful authors. Everything we know we learned from journeying with you through your careers.

Our blog readers, who ask hard questions, offer their own savvy insights, and expect us to show up every week with serious tips on how to make it through the publishing maze.

About the Authors

Janet Kobobel Grant had two goals as a grade-schooler: to read all the books in the library and to write a novel each summer. Her dream was to win the Pulitzer Prize. Well, she never did get all those books read, she seldom completed her summer writing project, and she certainly never won a Pulitzer Prize. But those unusual aspirations were indicative of her love of books.

She founded Books & Such Literary Management in 1996. The agency consists of five agents who represent more than 250 clients. Janet's clients include *New York Times* and *USA Today* best-selling authors and winners of the Holt Medallion and RITA. Previously she was a book editor for more than 12 years; an imprint editor at HarperCollins Christian Publishing; collaborator on seventeen books; and author of two books. As a result, Janet knows the publishing world from the perspective of a writer, an editor, and an agent.

Wendy Lawton feels equally comfortable in front of a computer, at a writers conference, or with a cool lump of clay in her hand. She's been an artist, a writer, and now for more than a decade, a literary agent and Vice President with the respected literary agency, Books & Such. Wendy represents many well-known authors including a *New York Times* #1 best-selling author.

For the first quarter century of her career, Lawton worked as a sculptor and doll designer. She began making dolls in 1979, founding The Lawton Doll Company of Turlock, California. In 2004, she received an honorary doctorate in arts and letters from Wilmington University in Delaware. In 2006 she was awarded the lifetime Achievement Award by *Dolls* Magazine.

She has served on the faculty of several major writers conferences, won the infamous Bulwer-Lytton competition, and has written thirteen of her own books along with a number of collaborations and ghostwritten books.

Made in the USA
Coppell, TX
21 May 2021